The Kingdom of the World

Politics Between God and the Devil

Robert L. Franck

Copyright © 2020 by Robert L. Franck

All rights reserved.

Scripture quotations are from The ESV® Bible (The Holy Bible, English Standard Version®), copyright © 2001 by Crossway, a publishing ministry of Good News Publishers. Used by permission. All rights reserved.

Cover Art: New Geographic and Hydrographic Map of the Whole World by Hendrik Hondius (1597-1651). Created in 1630. From Wikimedia Commons. The original was altered by shamelessly inserting the author's image over that of Geradus Mercator Flander.

ISBN-13: 979-8-6214-6336-6

For Lori

The most enduring woman
for the most boring man.

Yet it is not our part to master
all of the tides of the world,

but to do what is in us for the succor
of those years wherein we are set,

uprooting evil in the fields that we know,

so that those who live after
may have clean earth to till.[1]

Gandalf

---

[1] J.R.R. Tolkien, *The Return of the King*, (New York: Houghton Mifflin Company, 1994), 861.

Contents

Introduction 1

PART I—Understanding The Kingdom

1. Rulers, Rules and the Ruled 7
2. You May Speak 10
3. The First Principle 12
4. Rulers of Rulers 17
5. Ruler AND Ruled 25
6. Eternal Dominion 27
7. The Four Kingdoms 29
8. Neutral Ground 40
9. Kingdom Consolidation 44
10. Regarding the Church 50
11. Kingdom Confusion 53
12. Where Is the Church? 63

PART II—Living in The Kingdom

13. Joseph 71
14. Boaz 80
15. Obadiah 85
16. Jonah 92
17. Daniel 97
18. Esther 109
19. Paul 117
20. William Wilberforce 125
21. Dietrich Bonhoeffer 128
22. Lessons Learned 133

PART III—Justice and The Kingdom

23. Conscience and Justice 139
24. Religion and Justice 153
25. Love and Justice 170
26. Law and Justice 180

Conclusion 193
Acknowledgements 201

Introduction

I got this poster. I remember the verse on it.

> If my people who are called by my name humble themselves, and pray and seek my face and turn from their wicked ways, then I will hear from heaven and will forgive their sin and heal their land.
>
> II Chronicles 7:14

It was 1976, an election year. My first election. If voting was new to me, so was being a Christian. I was a toddler—two years old in the faith and full of wonder. I wondered, should a Christian vote? And, if so, for whom?

Jimmie Carter and Gerald Ford were the presidential candidates that year. Carter was the natural candidate for me. He unashamedly confessed that he was "born again." So was I. And as for Ford…well…he was the unelected incumbent that had succeeded the disgraced Richard Nixon.

* * *

I forget exactly where I got that poster. I may have bought it at a Christian book store. It may have been a freebie. No matter. The message was the important thing.

The poster, as I understood it, encouraged me to humble myself and confess my nation's sins—abortion and every other evil that I could think of. So I did. After all, wasn't there a promise here? IF…THEN…God would hear, forgive and heal the land. The land in question for me was the United States of America. So I was doing my part to help my country.

As I have matured in the faith I like to think that my grasp of the Scriptures has gotten firmer. Context, to begin with, is something to pay attention to. What is the context of II Chronicles 7:14? This promise was to King Solomon, in particular, and to the nation of Israel, in general. It was given within the larger context of God's covenant with Israel—a covenant that brought curses for disobedience and blessings for obedience.

What does a promise made specifically to the nation of Israel have to do with the United States? Well…not much. But even if it did, this verse would not provide much light on whether or not I should vote. Or for whom.

* * *

1976 was a year of stirring among Evangelicals—stirring from a season of hibernation from engagement with the larger society. It was not driven so much by a concern that the country was sliding toward Sodom and Gomorrah. We are always alarmed about that. But it was the growing consensus that we should take political action to do something about it. If the stirring began in 1976, the pot was fully boiling in 1980 with the emergence of the "Religious Right."

But the enthusiasm for political activism soon began to wane. Abortion remained legal and the slide toward Sodom and Gomorrah continued unabated. Some reconsidered. *We will never win hearts through politics. Only the gospel can change the culture. We have been branded as extremists! Politics was getting uncomfortably hot. Should we get out of the kitchen?*

This vacillation between enthusiasm and discouragement, between engagement and withdrawal, is not only a characteristics of Evangelicals. Christians throughout the history have disagreed over political involvement, with some taking one position and others the opposite. What is notable about Evangelicals is that we move relatively rapidly between the two options, swinging to one side and then to the other. Perhaps it is because we are more attuned to cultural currents. Perhaps it is because we are less grounded in tradition and theology.

And something bothers me about the argument that politics does not change hearts or culture. Whoever seriously thought that they would? Is that the purpose of politics? If not, what is the purpose? As for being called an "extremist," it is common political practice these days to label anyone who holds an opposing position an extremist. Does that mean I should not support or defend any position? What is at stake? What is my responsibility?

* * *

The particular dilemma about elections is that both voting and not voting have equal effect on a political outcome. Active participation empowers my influence. But I may be wrong. Passive avoidance multiplies the influence of others. But they may be wrong.

In 1976 I had to decide what I was going to do or not do. That is the way life is. I can wrestle with issues only so long before I must act. Life does not pause while I ponder.

I voted. For Ford.

* * *

While choosing which candidate to support had its difficulties, the real challenge was in the underlying issue. Should I vote? And when I dug beneath that question I found another. As a Christian, what is my relationship to government? And a little further. Should I participate in society for the common good? And further yet. How does all of this relate to the great spiritual struggle described in the Bible between good and evil, between God and Satan?

I could not fully articulate these deeper questions in 1976, much less attempt to answer them. But now I have more time to ponder than I did in the flurry of my youth. So out popped this book.

* * *

I begin at the bottom and work my way up, from principle to practice. The first part of this book is theological, providing a framework for understanding the world around you and your role in it. The second is biographical, a look at how godly people worked for good within the difficult political situations of their day. The third part is cultural, an evaluation of justice and its contemporary distortions.

This book is not about the election of 1976 or the last election or the next one. No living politician will be mentioned (except Mr. Carter, whom I will mention no more). To keep you from reacting instead of reflecting, I will avoid the hot button issues of today. My hope is that you will put aside all of the current tactical battles for the few hours it will take you to read this book in order to consider the strategic objectives.

So take a deep breath. Let go of your frustration, fear and, perhaps, rage. It is time to think.

Understanding the Kingdom
Part I

Your politics reveal a lot about you. Perhaps more than you know. They express what you really believe. And sometimes contradict what you say you believe.

Take, for example, your average culture-bred evolutionist. All is happenstance, according to the theory. If there is any meaning or purpose to life, it is the survival and advancement of the species. Everything serves this end. The strong should dominate the weak. The superior should subjugate the inferior. Yet the politics of many are just the opposite. They are for the oppressed and against the oppressors—as they should be, by the way. And they have been shocked by the policies of some of their fellow travelers who have been more consistent in their political applications.

But I'll pick on "them" later. I want to pick on you now.

You say that you believe the Bible. That is good. So do I. As it turns out, the Bible has much to say about politics. It is embedded throughout the entire book, although you probably have not looked at it from this perspective.

That is the problem. It is difficult to have your politics reflect your beliefs when you are unsure of your beliefs about politics.

I am here to help.

And even if we must agree to disagree on some points, I trust that you will gain a new appreciation for the scope and depth of biblical teaching about your roles and responsibilities in this world.

But the topic must first be defined before it can be explored.

1 Rulers, Rules and the Ruled

Every discussion should begin by clarifying the terms under discussion. What am I talking about? Do I really know? Do you? Am I babbling on about apples when you think the topic is oranges? That would be frustrating for both of us. I would think you a numbskull. You would consider me an idiot. So let's try to avoid this.

There is obviously a relationship between politics and government. In order to get us off on the right foot, here is what I mean when I use these words. Government is the social structure that establishes and enforces public order.

Imagine government as a coin. On one side are those who rule. These are the government officials. On the other side of the coin are those who are ruled. In our day these are the citizens. In the middle of the coin, holding the two sides together, are rules. Rules are the laws the rulers rule by. Force is the use of power to impose the rules. Compliance is the obedience of the ruled to the rules, whether voluntarily or under

compulsion.

Each of these elements is indispensable. If any one of them is eliminated government breaks down. Chaos follows. And since chaos is intolerable, it is soon replaced by another ruler with another set of rules. Any ruler. Any rules. It is better to be ruled by a despot under oppressive rules than to have no rules at all. In the first case, you can survive if you comply. In the second, there is only the Law of the Jungle—kill or be killed.

These are the most basic elements in every governmental system. Each particular system has additional complicating features. For example, there may be overlapping jurisdictions, which include city, county, state and national levels of government. There may be proliferation of rules, which make it impossible to know them all, much less obey them all. There may be voting, placing the responsibility of selecting the rulers on the ruled, which ultimately makes the ruled the rulers, I suppose. And there may be corruption, which tends to degrade the entire process.

So what then are politics? Politics are the persuasion, posturing, planning, pressuring, influencing, deal making, and shenanigans that surround government. In short, politics are the struggle over who gets to rule and what the rules will be.

Government and politics are inseparable. You cannot have one without the other. Like faith and works, they are different things but not separate things. To whip out some metaphors, government is the car and politics are the driver of the car. Government is a fish and politics are the ocean in which the fish swims. Government is the nail and politics are the hammer.

Because of the inseparability of government and politics, when I refer to one I mean that the other is tagging along. It would be tedious of me to write "government and politics" every time I use one term or the other. More to the point, it would detract from my concise and clever style of writing.

There is another thing about politics. Everyone must play the game. There is no way not to participate. It is a political act to comply with the rules. It is a political act to disobey the rules. It is a political act to change the rules or rulers, either by the rules, which is legal, or against the rules, which is rebellion. It is a political act to flee from a government in order to relocate under a better one. It is even a political act to refuse to participate in certain political acts like elections, because those who do not vote determine elections equally with those who do.

Like it or not, you are a politician in a broad sense. And this, my friend, creates all sorts of moral challenges and dilemmas for the Christian.

2 You May Speak

In my books I allow my readers to have a voice.
How gracious of you.
I am a humble man. Besides, you are more engaged if you are interacting with the content.
That seems helpful, but how will I know when I am saying something?
Your thoughts are typed in italics.
So they are.
Now you are catching on. Feel free to challenge anything I say. Iron sharpens iron.
Well then, I'll start with that first little chapter. I guess that this book is going to be a bunch of theory.
In overall purpose, yes. But I will also provide examples of how real people in real situations served God in difficult political circumstances.
That could actually be useful because the government sure seems to be getting more hostile to Christians and biblical morality.
While that is certainly true, I hope you will gain the perspective that most political situations throughout history have raised perplexing questions and placed God's people in very challenging predicaments. In fact, many situations have been much more difficult than yours.
Really?
Yes.
Maybe so, but things seem to be going from bad to worse. It is all so frustrating!
A little perspective is very calming medicine.
I can't be calm! I'm mad about these things!
Madness is not a mark of Christian maturity. Besides, without a proper foundation and realistic expectations, you are going to lurch between frantic activism and quitting in disgust. You will be a political manic-depressive—bipolar, as they now say.

Well…what's wrong with that?

It wastes a lot of time and energy, as well as keeping you confused and ineffective.

Hmmm. Let's get back to this dialog business. I have one condition.

What's that?

Promise that you won't always make me sound like an idiot.

I promise. Not always.

Okay.

3 The First Principle

A first principle is the most basic or foundational reason for doing something.

When I began writing *Buy A Cabin: The Theology and Practice of Rest* I was not thinking about the first principle of rest. Based on my experience I was thinking about the practical value of rest. Without rest you will become humorless, irritable, exhausted, ineffective and may eventually go insane. This was not a first principle but a description of the effects of not resting. But then I stumbled upon the first principle. It was cleverly obscured at the beginning of the Bible.

> And on the seventh day God finished his work that he had done, and he rested on the seventh day from all his work that he had done.
>
> Genesis 2:2

The first principle of rest is that God rests! That revelation was the basis for all that followed in my book. You are made in God's image and, therefore, you are to rest. Rest is good. Rest is a blessing. Etc. Read the book for yourself. I am not going to repeat it all here.

The topic of this book is political involvement. What is the first principle for political involvement?

Ummm.

Consider the history of Christianity. Since all Christians have had to deal with politics—often as a matter of life or death—you would think that it would be addressed in the significant documents of the faith. What do the great creeds and confessions say about politics? Unfortunately not much.

The reason is that the creeds and confessions are reactive. Reactive to what? To heresies and disagreements within the faith and attacks from outside the faith. We must be threatened, it seems, by a wrong answer before articulating a right answer. For better or worse, there has never been a major controversy over political involvement. Most Christians just accept their political roles and opportunities, whatever they happen to be at the time without thinking much about them. There have been controversies over the Trinity, the nature of Christ, the relationship between faith and works, and church government but not about politics.

To be fair, the issue has not been completely ignored. You may find it addressed in the recesses of various systematic theologies. And something else may have been bouncing around inside your cranium during this discussion—the first question and answer of the Westminster Shorter Catechism.

> Q. What is the chief end of man?
> A. Man's chief end is to glorify God, and to enjoy him forever.

There is much to be commended here. It addresses purpose and correctly summarizes the proper relationship between man and God. Everything about it is rich and right. But…it is also somewhat abstract. A practical person may respond: *Obviously true. But how am I supposed to do that?* This practical person may be told that he is not cut out for seminary or that he should dedicate himself to pious religious exercises. But the practical person has a point. The broad goal of glorifying God provides little specific guidance on why you should or should not vote, for instance.

At this point I could appeal to my strong feelings, my brilliant opinions, a clever story, some historical lessons, or even claim that I have had a vision. But none of these arguments should persuade you. Something more authoritative is needed.

Look in the Book

As a last resort in this quest for the first principle of politics, let me turn again to the Bible. Here is the answer that will satisfy both the theologian and the practical person—the theologian because it is…well…biblical and the practical person because it is…well…practical. And like the first principle for rest, it is hidden right at the beginning.

> Then God said, "Let us make man in our image, after our likeness. And let them have **dominion** over the fish of the sea and over the birds of the heavens and over the livestock and over all the earth and over every creeping thing that creeps on the earth." So God created man in

> his own image, in the image of God he created him; male and female he created them. And God blessed them. And God said to them, "Be fruitful and multiply and fill the earth and subdue it, and have **dominion** over the fish of the sea and over the birds of the heavens and over every living thing that moves on the earth."
> Genesis 1:26-28

This passage is known as the Dominion Mandate or the Cultural Mandate. The Dominion Mandate seems to be the better description, since "dominion" is the repeated theme not "culture." (Sometimes it is better to stick with the text than to discover some more profound but unintended meaning.) Dominion involves reigning, i.e. exercising authority and control. It is ruling or governing. From the context it is apparent that God has dominion over all things because he created them. Whoever makes something owns it and can do with it as he pleases.

The final act of creation is man, that is, the human race. Unlike the rest of creation, God makes man in his image. Man is not God but he is like God in some ways. One of the ways is work. God's work is dominion and man's work is delegated dominion. Man does not own the earth, of course, but the Owner assigns and entrusts him to exercise dominion over it. Man is the steward of the earth. Ruling the earth is his job. In sum, man is under God and over the earth, like this:

The big crown symbolizes God's ruling authority by right of creation. The little crown symbolizes the authority God delegated to man to rule over the earth. The stickman here represents the entire human race. While it is true that each individual is accountable to God for his particular dominion roles, mankind as a whole has the overall responsibility for ruling the earth.

The Dominion Mandate is described in the first chapter of Genesis and applied in the second chapter. Adam is placed in the Garden of Eden to "work it and keep it" (2:15). God then brings the animals to Adam so that he can name them (2:19-20). The first man begins the first exercises of dominion over the land and the living creatures. But the job is too big for one man alone.

> Then the LORD God said, "It is not good that the man should be alone; I will make him a helper fit for him."
> Genesis 2:18

God creates Eve, a wife for Adam. Together they and all who will come from them are to "be fruitful and multiply and fill the earth and subdue it" in order to fulfill God's purpose for them.

Trouble in Paradise

Man had one specific restriction, one rule. God had every right to make this rule. Although man was over the earth, he was under God's overall dominion. Adam was not an autonomous being. And neither are you as a member of Adam's race. This was the restriction.

> And the LORD God commanded the man, saying, "You may surely eat of every tree of the garden, but of the tree of the knowledge of good and evil you shall not eat, for in the day that you eat of it you shall surely die."
> Genesis 2:16-17

Unfortunately for Adam and Eve and every one of their descendants, they violated this rule in the very next chapter. They rebelled against God. There were many consequences of their action. All involved suffering, culminating in spiritual and physical death. The woman would now experience pain in childbirth (3:16). There would be hurt in multiplying and filling the earth. The man would now earn his bread through toil, sweat and pain (3:17-19). The entire earth—the domain of the human race and the race itself—was cursed.

But here is an amazing thing. Although man's domain had been corrupted by sin and the human race itself was corrupted, the Dominion Mandate remained unaltered. God did not revoke the mandate. The human race is still responsible to rule the earth.

Picture a man in rebellion against an earthly king. The fact of the king's authority is not altered by the rebel's refusal to submit to that authority. The rebel is still responsible to follow the king's rules. If he has broken the rules, the rebel must either be reconciled to the king or receive the penalty of his disobedience.

Evangelicals understand this imagery. All are rebels against the rightful rule of God. Jesus—the Son of God, God himself—forgives your rebellion when you repent and believe. Jesus pays your penalty and reconciles you to God. The alternative outcome is that the rebel is sentenced for his transgressions at the last judgement. And the penalty is steep indeed—rebellion against a holy eternal God is eternal punishment from God.

This understanding of eternal destiny is correct, of course, but is often divorced from the context of the Dominion Mandate. It is seen as a matter to be settled apart from any connection to the earth. However, as you will see shortly, what you have done on the earth, your earthiness—your body—and your future role on the earth are all inseparable from God's purposes for mankind for eternity.

But I am jumping ahead in the dominion story. So far I have only established that sinful man still retains dominion responsibilities and accountability even though he is in rebellion against God.

Up to this point in Genesis, man's dominion has been identified as rule over land and animals. But what about people ruling over other people?

That is a question for the next chapter.

4 Rulers of Rulers

Before the end of third chapter of Genesis people are exercising dominion—authority and rule—over other people.

The Family

And in what is certain to cause teeth gnashing to modern sensibilities, human over human dominion is first applied within families.

> To the woman he said...your desire shall be for your husband, and he shall **rule** over you.
> Genesis 3:16

"He shall rule over you." The husband is to rule his wife. This is the concept of "headship." The wife is to submit to her husband.

This dominion institution is singled out nowadays as being intolerably oppressive. *This is the continuation of the historic exploitation of women by men!* While some men have tyrannized some women in marriage (just as some women have tyrannized some men in marriage), it does not follow that the ruler-ruled relationship must now be discarded. No. The order God has established does not cause sin. It is designed for your good. The sin lies with those who abuse their position, not because they have a position. And the ruled can abuse their position just as the rulers can.

There is another ruler-ruled relationship within the family. The parents are to rule over their children. Children are to obey their parents. Is this also an oppressive arrangement? *This is the continuation of the historic exploitation of children by parents!* Fortunately, most people still have enough association with the realities of child rearing to know that the two-year-old son or the thirteen-year-old daughter should not have an equal voice with the parents in family governance. Those who don't know this and fail to learn it will…how shall I describe it…encounter a great deal of frustration and disappointment.

In short, there is a hierarchy of authority within the family structure. It is a small dominion. It is one aspect of the larger Dominion Mandate. I will picture the family dominion relationships as a house, like so:

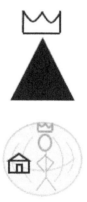

And that is not the only ruler-ruled relationship.

Employment

The second dominion institution is that which is described in the Scripture as the master-servant relationship.

> Bondservants, obey your earthly masters with fear and trembling, with a sincere heart, as you would Christ, not by the way of eye-service, as people-pleasers, but as bondservants of Christ, doing the will of God from the heart, rendering service with a good will as to the Lord and not to man, knowing that whatever good anyone does, this he will receive back from the Lord, whether he is a bondservant or is free.
>
> Ephesians 6:5-8

Servants are to "obey" their masters "as you would Christ." This is a high standard that encompasses inward motivation as well as outward action. Why? Because you ultimately serve God by serving your dominion rulers.

Is service to the master to be absolute and unquestioning? Let me just say for now that obedience is qualified in this passage. "Whatever good anyone does." The requirement to serve the master as you would Jesus assumes that the master is requiring what is good.

Does this only apply to slavery? No, it doesn't. Note the last phrase. "Bondservant or free." That net is wide enough to catch your employment situation, so don't try to claim an exemption here.

Is the only obligation on the ruled? No. Like all dominion relationships, the rulers have responsibilities as well as the ruled.

> Masters, do the same to them, and stop your threatening, knowing that he who is both their Master and yours is in heaven, and that there is no partiality with him.
>
> Ephesians 6:9

In fact, Jesus had something to say about masters.

> And Jesus called them to him and said to them, "You know that those who are considered rulers of the Gentiles lord it over them, and their great ones exercise authority over them. But it shall not be so among you. But whoever would be great among you must be your servant, and whoever would be first among you must be slave of all. For even the Son of Man came not to be served but to serve, and to give his life as a ransom for many."
>
> Mark 10:42-45

Jesus, as he often did, turned conventional wisdom on its head. The temptation in this fallen world is to use a ruling position to exploit the ruled. Many do not resist this temptation. But Jesus' followers must use their positions of ruling to serve those whom they rule. The master is to wash the feet of the servant. This same principle applies across all dominion institutions. The husband is to love the wife. The magistrate is to be "God's servant for your good." But now I am leaping ahead.

Since employment relationships today involve the earning of money for service these days, I will add the dollar sign to symbolize the relationship.

THE KINGDOM OF THE WORLD

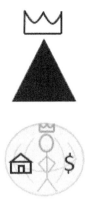

I like your clever little illustration. But you are wandering. Are you ever going to get back on the subject of politics?

Yes, politics are next. And you should be noticing a pattern emerging in these dominion relationships. Ruler-ruled dynamics all work the same way. These birds fly together and their direction is easiest to follow when you watch the whole flock.

Government

Now to the third dominion institution. Government. What does God require from you in relation to government? This is not an easy question to answer because there are such a wide variety of government forms—not only throughout history but within the Bible itself. But do not be overwhelmed by the various expressions of government or their surrounding politics. Focus on what are the common responsibilities of all of them. The Apostle Paul tells us exactly what these are in the most extensive and definitive passage on government in Scripture.

> Let every person be subject to the governing authorities. For there is no authority except from God, and those that exist have been instituted by God. Therefore whoever resists the authorities resists what God has appointed, and those who resist will incur judgment. For rulers are not a terror to good conduct, but to bad. Would you have no fear of the one who is in authority? Then do what is good, and you will receive his approval, for he is God's servant for your good. But if you do wrong, be afraid, for he does not bear the sword in vain. For he is the servant of God, an avenger who carries out God's wrath on the wrongdoer. Therefore one must be in subjection, not

> only to avoid God's wrath but also for the sake of conscience. For because of this you also pay taxes, for the authorities are ministers of God, attending to this very thing. Pay to all what is owed to them: taxes to whom taxes are owed, revenue to whom revenue is owed, respect to whom respect is owed, honor to whom honor is owed.
>
> Romans 13:1-7

Some observations. To begin with, you are to submit to the governing authorities. Just as in the institutions of family and employment, the ruled are to obey the rulers. Why? Because there is "no authority except from God, and those that exist have been instituted by God." Human authority was established by God. He delegated ruling authority to the human race as a whole in the Dominion Mandate. But it is also clear from this passage that every human ruler possesses God's authority by God's sovereign appointment.

Does this mean that disobedience to rulers is the same as disobedience to God? Does this mean that a ruler rules *as* God? No, it does not. Note carefully the wording here. "Therefore whoever resists the authorities resists what God has appointed." The appointee is not the appointer. However, the appointee is responsible to carry out the will of the appointer.

Authority comes with a commission. What is that commission? Rulers are to be a "terror…to bad conduct." That is, rulers should punish evildoers. Justice is required. Punishment is symbolized by the sword—the ultimate exercise of government authority, which is execution.

So then, is government merely a negative function, a punisher of evildoers, a yielder of the sword? No, it is not. While this is a primary function of government, it is not the only function. Does your government only consist of a police force, criminal courts and prisons? No, it does not. Government is responsible for all aspects of civil order. Governors, mayors, town councils, school boards, etc. are government rulers too.

Rulers are not only to punish bad behavior but to encourage good behavior. This is clear from the passage. "Rulers are not a terror to good conduct. Then do what is good, and you will receive his approval. He is God's servant for your good." Good. Good. Good. There is a positive as well as a negative function.

Because of the full range of responsibilities for the common good—community infrastructure, fair and orderly commerce, national defense, etc.—you are commanded to: "Pay to all what is owed to them: taxes to whom taxes are owed, revenue to whom revenue is owed, respect to whom respect is owed, honor to whom honor is owed." A government ruler is a "servant" and "minister" of God, as well as being an "avenger" of God.

But…what about rulers that are wicked and encourage evil behavior instead of good? You keep avoiding that. Am I obligated to submit to them?

I knew you were going to ask that.

Well, what about it? You may have noticed that there is quite a bit of corruption in government. Does that release me from my obligation to obey?

That is the big question. I will tackle it in the next section of this book when we look at godly people who were placed in such circumstances. But in the Romans passage Paul does not address the issue of disobedience to rulers. He only described the basis of their authority and the requirement to submit to them, which is in the context of exercising their intended functions.

Exceptions to obedience aside, I am trying to build a general model that depicts the biblical teaching about the dominion institutions. So I will add government (symbolized by the gavel and sword) to my clever little illustration, as you call it.

Now, have I constructed this model by cherry picking a few phrases out of the Scripture to prove my point? Let's see.

Show Time!

Consider the Apostle Paul's letter to the Colossians. What does he have to say about dominion responsibilities?

> Wives, submit to your husbands, as is fitting in the Lord. Husbands, love your wives, and do not be harsh with them. Children, obey your parents in everything, for this pleases the Lord. Fathers, do not provoke your children, lest they become discouraged. Bondservants, obey in everything those who are your earthly masters, not by

> way of eye-service, as people-pleasers, but with sincerity of heart, fearing the Lord. Whatever you do, work heartily, as for the Lord and not for men, knowing that from the Lord you will receive the inheritance as your reward. You are serving the Lord Christ.
>
> Colossians 3:18-24

Paul upholds the ruler-ruled relationships in the institutions of family and employment. He omits government, perhaps because he covered it so thoroughly in Romans chapter thirteen.

But the Apostle Peter, begins with government and covers all three institutions in his first letter.

> Be subject for the Lord's sake to **every human institution**, whether it be to the emperor as supreme, or to governors as sent by him to punish those who do evil and to praise those who do good. For this is the will of God, that by doing good you should put to silence the ignorance of foolish people. Live as people who are free, not using your freedom as a cover-up for evil, but living as servants of God. Honor everyone. Love the brotherhood. Fear God. Honor the emperor. Servants, be subject to your masters with all respect, not only to the good and gentle but also to the unjust. ...Likewise, wives, be subject to your own husbands....
>
> 1 Peter 2:13-18; 3:1

In context, these two passages are the application that flows from what was written before. What was that? You can easily find out by reading Colossians and I Peter. But I'll summarize for you. The apostles begin these books by describing the spiritual blessings you have in Jesus.

Do you see the connection? Spiritual realities should motivate you to fulfill your physical responsibilities. While some throughout the history of the church have taught the truly "spiritual" person should withdraw from their dominion duties, the apostles taught the opposite. I'll stick with the apostles on this one. You should too.

Now connect the dots. Why should you embrace your political, employment and family roles? It is not because you are a Christian. It is because you are a human. You do not stop being a human when you repent and believe the Gospel. You do not somehow mystically transcended God's purpose for mankind to rule the earth. But you should become a certain type of person—a person that honors God in the way you fulfill your dominion responsibilities.

I am not saying that Christians must meet a higher standard. God has only one standard for righteous living. It is the standard that everyone will be measured by when bowing before Jesus at the last judgement. But there are a number of additional reasons that should motivate every Christian. The Apostle Paul includes them in his dominion exhortations to Titus.

> ...that the word of God may not be reviled.
>
> Titus 2:5

> ...so that an opponent may be put to shame, having nothing evil to say about us.
>
> Titus 2:8

> ...so that in everything they may adorn the doctrine of God our Savior.
>
> Titus 2:10

> ...I want you to insist on these things, so that those who have believed in God may be careful to devote themselves to good works. These things are excellent and profitable for people.
>
> Titus 3:8

Your dominion behavior reflects directly on your Christian witness. Do it well and God is honored. Mess it up and all that you profess to be true is discredited by your actions. Unbelievers do not separate your faith from your actions...and neither should you. What you do displays who you are.

And everyone knows it. The most striking thing about the above passage is that Titus assumes the morality of your actions are self-evident. People know when your behavior is good and when it is evil. Why is that? Because we have all been created by the same God and are subject to the same standards.

To summarize, your dominion responsibilities are not some hidden, secret biblical wisdom that has been brilliantly unveiled by me. No. I am simply pointing out a major biblical theme that should be obvious to all.

5 Ruler AND Ruled

Now back to the drawing board. Think of all of the people you are connected to in ruler-ruled relationships. In some you are the ruler and in some you are the ruled.

The child grows up and becomes a parent. The employee is promoted to manager…but still has a boss. The citizen is elected to the town council. And there are additional relationships—like teacher-student and coach-player—that fall under the three major dominion institutions. In short, you are embedded in a multi-layered ruler-ruled hierarchy, like so:

This illustration is simplified for clarity. In actuality you have many more ruler-ruled relationships than this few number. But I weary of drawing more little stick men stacked high and low, layer upon layer, so you must multiply them yourself in your imagination.

* * *

That's it? That's all you've got for a chapter?

A little chapter is like an unexpected treat. It gives you a sense of accomplishment that you don't really deserve. So take the rest of the night off. Read that exciting novel. Watch a show or a game.

But don't worry. You'll pay for this. I've got some long chapters coming up.

6 Eternal Dominion

To wrap up my survey of the dominion theme, let's go to the end of the Bible to complete the picture. I suspect that you may think that man's dominion over the earth is a temporary gig. Ruling the earth is only your duty until your soul flies up to an immaterial paradise where you will strum a golden harp amongst the ethereal clouds.

Well....

Let's look at the biblical description.

> Then I saw a new heaven and a new earth, for the first heaven and the first earth had passed away, and the sea was no more. And I saw the holy city, new Jerusalem, coming down out of heaven from God, prepared as a bride adorned for her husband. And I heard a loud voice from the throne saying, "Behold, the dwelling place of God is with man. He will dwell with them, and they will be his people, and God himself will be with them as their God.
>
> Revelation 21:1-3

While there is much to ponder here, I will only sketch out the parallels between the account in Genesis and this vision in Revelation. In Genesis God creates the heavens and the earth. In Revelation these have passed away and God replaces them with a new heaven and earth. The beginning scene in Genesis is in a garden on the earth. The final scene in Revelation is in a city, the New Jerusalem, which will come down from heaven to earth. In Genesis man's fall brings a curse. In Revelation the Lamb (Jesus) removes the curse. In Genesis God is present on the earth—he walks and talks with Adam. In Revelation God dwells with man on the earth, he is their light, and he rules over them from his throne.

And what of the Dominion Mandate? Will it be superseded by the presence of God? No, it will not. Revelation concludes with a description of the river of the water of life and the tree of life and this:

> No longer will there be anything accursed, but the throne of God and of the Lamb will be in it, and his **servants** will worship him. They will see his face, and his name will be on their foreheads. And night will be no more. They will need no light of lamp or sun, for the Lord God will be their light, and **they will reign** forever and ever.
> Revelation 22:3-5

The redeemed on the New Earth are called "his servants." Servants serve. And what is this service? It is to "reign forever and ever." Reign over what? Over the earth. The redeemed will fulfill what has always been God's purpose for Adam's race—exercising dominion rule over the earth.

Jesus anticipated this repeatedly during his earthly ministry. He promised that the meek shall inherit the earth (Matthew 5:5). In the parables of the talents (Matthew 25) and the minas (Luke 19) faithfulness in this world results in a reward of more responsibility in the world to come. In Matthew the reward is to be "set over much." In Luke it is to have authority over "cities." Doesn't that sound like dominion to you?

I guess.

So then, from creation through eternity these three things are inseparable: people, ruling and earth. The point of having connected these dots is so you will understand how politics fits into the larger context of your dominion responsibilities.

* * *

This is all very interesting but if this dominion business is so clear in the Bible, why don't I hear more about it?

That's a good question.
So answer it.

7 The Four Kingdoms

To understanding your responsibilities in this world, including politics, you must first grasp the various aspects of the Bible's kingdom teaching. Define the kingdoms correctly and your dominion responsibilities become clear.

The Everlasting Kingdom

The first kingdom concept in Scripture, as you may have guessed, is God's universal rule. I will call this "over-rule." The kingdom through which God exercises over-rule is termed the "everlasting kingdom" in this passage.

> Your kingdom is an **everlasting kingdom**, and
> your **dominion** endures throughout all generations.
> Psalm 145:13

Note that "kingdom" and "dominion" are used in parallel, showing that the terms mean the same thing.[2] Also, let me point out something else that is obvious. Everlasting means always and forever. So if there are other kingdoms (which there are), they must operate within the everlasting kingdom, as do the rulers, rules and ruled of those kingdoms.

I could quote passage after passage about God's over-rule, but I trust that you read the Bible on your own and have already mastered the concept that God is actually God. He is the Supreme Ruler. Everyone and everything are subject to his sovereign rule. He brings his plans and purposes to fulfillment.

I had already placed a big crown over God by right of creation. Now

---

[2] Parallelism is a common feature in Hebrew poetry. In this passage the second line repeats the idea in the first, which is synonymous parallelism.

you know that it is also there by right of his kingship over his everlasting kingdom.

Psalm 145 continues and describes God's rule over his everlasting kingdom, including this phrase.

> The LORD is righteous in all his ways....
>
> Psalm 145:17

God's character is expressed through his rule. In addition to his righteousness, I could add his love and his justice, as well as his other attributes. What God does is perfectly consistent with who God is.

But if God is sovereign over his all-encompassing kingdom, why is there evil in the world? And what should be done about it? These are the great questions that all religions and philosophies attempt to answer.

The Bible's answer is found by understanding the other kingdoms. There are three more.

The Kingdom of the World

The second kingdom concept is, of course, the subject of this book—man's rule, including human government. The Bible refers to this kingdom both in the plural, the "kingdoms of the world,"[3] and in the singular, the "kingdom of the world."[4] The book of Daniel also refers to government in the singular as the "kingdom of men."[5]

That "world" and "men" are used interchangeably should come as no surprise. The world, or the earth, is the domain of man. It is the human kingdom subdivided into a multitude of rulerships. For consistency throughout this book, I will refer to all human governments as the "kingdom of the world."

In order to distinguish human responsibility from God's sovereign rule, I will coin a second term. "Under-rule." Get it? God exercises over-rule. Man exercises under-rule.

This is the little crown depicting man's dominion rule over the earth, which in a kingdom context symbolizes his kingship over the kingdom of the world.

Now what is the relationship of the kingdom of the world (man's under-rule) to the everlasting kingdom (God's over-rule)? In the following passage Nebuchadnezzar, ruler of Babylonian, is put on notice that he is going to find out.

---

[3] See Isaiah 23:17, Jeremiah 25:26, Matthew 4:8 and Luke 4:5.
[4] See Revelation 11:15.
[5] See Daniel 4:17,25 and 32.

> You [Nebuchadnezzar] shall be made to eat grass like an ox, and you shall be wet with the dew of heaven, and seven periods of time shall pass over you, till you know that the Most High rules the **kingdom of men** and gives it to whom he will.
>
> Daniel 4:25

No surprise here. God in his over-rule appoints and deposes of under-ruling humans at will. Because of Nebuchadnezzar's pride, he had to learn this lesson the hard way—via the bovine treatment. When he finally comes to his senses, he acknowledges the sovereignty of God.

Two errors deny this truth. One is that if God over-rules, then man does not really under-rule. The other is that if man under-rules, then God does not really over-rule. The first makes man less than man as the ruler of the earth. The second makes God less than God as ruler of the everlasting kingdom, subjecting him to man's will in some convoluted way.

But man is not a robot and God actually is God. Understanding the kingdoms will help you hold on to both of these truths, one in each hand.

Now concerning evil in the kingdom of the world. Man and his realm were corrupted when he sinned in the garden. But the Dominion Mandate was not rescinded. The human race is still to rule over the earth and, significantly, God still requires that rule to reflect his character, his image. That is, government should be executed with righteousness, love and justice.

This requirement is seen throughout the Bible. You can find examples everywhere in both the Old and New Testaments, as thick as cherries on a cherry tree. I have picked the two below as a sample.

> Hate evil, and love good, and establish justice in the gate.
>
> Amos 5:15

> He has told you, O man, what is good; and what does the LORD require of you but to do justice, and to love kindness, and to walk humbly with your God?
>
> Micah 6:8

But what should be done is not always done. Rulers sin. So do the ruled. And there are evil rules. This is our experience in the kingdom of the world. Why is all of this happening? Simply, man is a sinner and the corruption of politics are the result.

But there is also more going on than meets the eye.

And Jesus came to earth to explain it.

The Kingdom of God

Jesus was always talking about kingdom. His introductory remarks to his public ministry were:

> The time is fulfilled, and the **kingdom of God** is at hand; repent and believe in the gospel.
>
> Mark 1:15

Did you notice the parallelism between "kingdom of God" and "gospel?" Other passages use the phrase "gospel of the kingdom," which is the good news of the kingdom. Interesting. What exactly is this third kingdom?

Whatever it is, the kingdom of God was a very controversial topic with the Jewish leaders. Why? Because Jesus' words and works were a threat to their social position. The conflict between them centered around the word "authority," which is a kingdom word, a dominion word. Did Jesus have the authority—the right and power—to say what he was saying and do what he was doing? Apparently so. He taught with authority. He healed with authority. He cast out demons with authority. And he claimed the authority to do the one thing most crucial to the kingdom of God.

That one thing was revealed in an event. Jesus was teaching. People were coming to be healed. A paralyzed man could not come to be healed because…er…he was paralyzed, so his friends carried him. They could not reach Jesus because of the crowds surrounding him. So they went up on the roof, made a hole through it and lowered the man down. Then something unexpected happened. Jesus said, "Your sins are forgiven you."

The scribes and Pharisees charged him with blasphemy. Their reasoning was that only God had the authority to forgive sins. This was right. But Jesus did not have the authority of God, they claimed. This was wrong.

> But that you may know that the Son of Man has **authority** on earth to **forgive sins**"—he said to the man who was paralyzed—"I say to you, rise, pick up your bed and go home."
>
> Luke 5:24

Jesus' power to heal validated his authority to forgive sins. The forgiveness of sins is the gospel, the good news. It is the central concept of the kingdom of God. That is why it is included in the central prayer of the kingdom, the Lord's prayer.

> Forgive us our debts, as we also have forgiven our debtors.
>
> Matthew 6:12

And in this verse you also find an example of the rules in the kingdom of God. The forgiven are to forgive. The ruled are to reflect the character of their Ruler.

However, the Jewish leadership rejected Jesus' kingdom teaching. They accepted only Moses' teaching…as understood through their traditions. They would abide neither the message nor the messenger of this kingdom of God. Jesus must be destroyed.

To achieve this end, the Jewish leaders devised a political dirty trick. To kill Jesus required the cooperation of the Roman government. Only the government could perform capital punishment. What would compel the government to execute a man who healed the sick and preached about the forgiveness of sin? Not much there, really.

So they worked a different angle—a political angle. They accused Jesus of insurrection, of plotting to overthrow the Roman state. In other words, they claimed that his intention was to establish a kingdom of the world not the kingdom of God.

> And they began to accuse him, saying, "We found this man misleading our nation and forbidding us to give tribute to Caesar, and saying that he himself is Christ, a king."
>
> Luke 23:2

When the Roman governor expressed skepticism over these charges, they pulled out all the stops.

> Pilate said to them, "Shall I crucify your King?" The chief priests answered, "We have no king but Caesar."
>
> John 19:15

"We have no king but Caesar?" It is hard to imagine a more deceitful thing for these Jews to say. Yet they were willing to commit political prostitution in order to obtain Jesus' death. (This type of chicanery is what gives politics such a bad name.) But Jesus had always distinguished between the kingdom of the world and the kingdom of God.

> Therefore render to Caesar the things that are Caesar's, and to God the things that are God's.
>
> Matthew 22:21

And when asked directly by Pilate about his kingship, he replied:

> My kingdom is not of this world. If my kingdom were of this world, my servants would have been fighting, that I might not be delivered over to the Jews. But my kingdom is not from the world.
>
> John 18:36

Jesus said that his kingdom was not a kingdom of the world, not a political kingdom, not a kingdom with an army, not a physical kingdom like other nations at all. Jesus' kingdom was different from these.

Then the Roman governor raised the issue of authority—his own political authority. In response, Jesus reminded him where that authority came from.

> So Pilate said to him, "You will not speak to me? Do you not know that I have **authority** to release you and authority to crucify you?" Jesus answered him, "You would have no **authority** over me at all unless it had been given you from above."
>
> John 19:10-11

But there is something more astounding here than Jesus' affirmation of the everlasting kingdom, of the sovereignty of God. Did you catch it? In the same sentence that Jesus spoke of God's sovereign authority over Pilate, he acknowledged Pilate's human authority over him.

What kind of kingdom is the kingdom of God? Unlike the kingdom of the world, this kingdom is an invisible kingdom.

> Being asked by the Pharisees when the kingdom of God would come, he answered them, "The **kingdom of God is not coming in ways that can be observed**, nor will they say, 'Look, here it is!' or 'There!' for behold, the kingdom of God is in the midst of you."
>
> Luke 17:20-21

Jesus also uses the analogy of wind. You cannot see the wind but you see the effects of the wind. It is present and powerful but unseen.

> The wind blows where it wishes, and you hear its sound, but you do not know where it comes from or where it goes. So it is with everyone who is born of the Spirit.
>
> John 3:8

This aspect of invisibility reveals the very nature of the kingdom of God. It is a *spiritual* kingdom. That is, it is non-physical, non-material. In fact, the Bible contrasts the spiritual and the physical. The spiritual is described as "unseen" while the physical is "seen."

> Now faith is the assurance of things hoped for, the conviction of things **not seen**.
>
> Hebrews 11:1

Faith, then, is described as seeing the unseen. It is believing what God has said and acting accordingly, as Moses did.

> By faith he left Egypt, not being afraid of the anger of the king, for he endured as **seeing** him who is **invisible**.
>
> Hebrews 11:27

But the kingdom of God is not the only unseen kingdom. There is another one.

The Kingdom of Satan

This fourth and last kingdom is a rival spiritual kingdom. Like the kingdom of God, it was largely hidden in the Old Testament. There are glimpses of it here and there. But it is not fully revealed until Jesus described it.

This kingdom has a different ruler.

> But when the Pharisees heard it, they said, "It is only by **Beelzebul**, the prince of demons, that this man casts out demons." Knowing their thoughts, he [Jesus] said to them, "Every kingdom divided against itself is laid waste, and no city or house divided against itself will stand. And if **Satan** casts out Satan, he is divided against himself. How then will his **kingdom** stand?"
>
> Matthew 12:24-26

Different rules.

> By this it is evident who are the children of God, and who are the children of the devil: **whoever does not practice righteousness** is not of God, nor is the one who does not love his brother.
>
> I John 3:10

And different ruled.

> You are of **your father the devil**, and your will is to do your father's desires. He was a murderer from the beginning, and does not stand in the truth, because there is no truth in him. When he lies, he speaks out of his own character, for he is a liar and the father of lies.
>
> John 8:44

Who are the ruled in Satan's kingdom? The children of the devil. Interestingly, this relationship is described in *family* terminology not *citizenship* terminology. But if you think about it, so is the kingdom of God. God is our Ruler but also our Father. Jesus is our Lord but also our Brother. So then, the kingdoms have a family aspect to them. I could chase this theme further, but if I did you would probably lose the main trail.

The point is, every person belongs in either one or the other of these spiritual kingdoms—the kingdom of Satan or the kingdom of God. Salvation, then, is simply moving out of the former and into the latter.

> He [God the Father] has delivered us from the **domain of darkness** and **transferred** us to the **kingdom of his beloved Son**, in whom we have redemption, the forgiveness of sins.
>
> Colossians 1:13-14

This is the gospel, the good news.

There is one last question about this fourth kingdom? What is its relationship to the first one? Does Satan operate outside of the sovereignty of God? Is he an equal or a balancing power? No, he is not. He is a rebel against God's authority, but he cannot escape it. This is evident in the opening scene in the book of Job.

> Now there was a day when the sons of God came to present themselves before the LORD, and Satan also came among them. The LORD said to Satan, "From where have you come?" Satan answered the LORD and said, "From going to and fro on the earth, and from walking up

THE KINGDOM OF THE WORLD

> and down on it." And the LORD said to Satan, "Have you considered my servant Job...."
>
> Job 1:6-8

Satan presents himself to God—the lesser to the greater, the ruled before the ruler, the created under the creator. Then he asks for permission to tempt Job, which God grants within defined limits. At the end of the book we read that while Satan meant to destroy Job, God sovereignly accomplishes his good purpose. Even the kingdom of Satan operates within the everlasting kingdom.

Pulling It Together

In summary, God has appointed mankind to rule over the earth. This work is organized and structured through the institutions of family, employment and government.

Switching to kingdom terminology, government is the kingdom of the world. The Bible describes three additional kingdoms—the everlasting kingdom, the kingdom of God and the kingdom of Satan. The kingdom of the world is a physical kingdom. The kingdoms of God and Satan are spiritual kingdoms. The everlasting kingdom is a universal kingdom, enveloping both the spiritual and physical kingdoms.

Here is the whole picture.

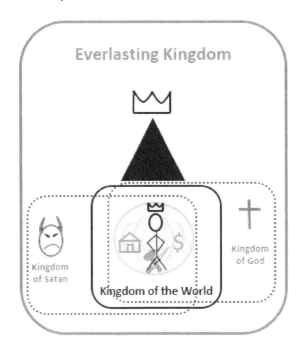

You live under the rule of three of the four kingdoms. You are obviously in the everlasting kingdom, subject to the sovereign rule of God along with all else that exists. You are in the kingdom of the world, subject to human government rulers. And you are in one or the other of the spiritual kingdoms subject to either the rule of Satan or of Jesus, depending on which one you are following.

Dual Citizenship

What has confused Christians throughout the centuries is the idea that because you are in the kingdom of God, you are no longer in the kingdom of the world. It is one OR the other. This is a false choice. But at first glance, this verse seems to validate it.

> But our citizenship is in heaven....
>
> Philippians 3:20

This passage describes your relationship to the kingdom of God not in family terminology but in government terminology. But the contrast here is not between the kingdom of God and the kingdom of the world. It is not pitting your spiritual citizenship against your physical citizenship. It is contrasting the kingdom of God with the kingdom of Satan.

Here is the verse again. This time in context.

> For many, of whom I have often told you and now tell you even with tears, walk as enemies of the cross of Christ. Their end is destruction, their god is their belly, and they glory in their shame, with minds set on earthly things. But our citizenship is in heaven....
>
> Philippians 3:18-20

The OR choice is between the spiritual kingdoms. The Apostle Paul is warning the Philippians about those who are "enemies of the cross of Christ." Who are these people? They are citizens of the kingdom of Satan. It is their spiritual allegiance not their national allegiance that is Paul's concern.

Besides, do you really think that the Apostle would tell you repeatedly to honor and obey your political rulers and then contradict himself by saying you have no responsibilities to the government? No. Christians are citizens of heaven AND citizens of nations.

8 Neutral Ground

It is amazing how the biblical concept of the kingdoms provides such a practical understanding of your roles and responsibilities in this world. Instead of seeking to avoid them through some higher level of "spirituality" or mystical enlightenment, you may wholeheartedly embrace them. They are not a distraction from your walk with God. They are the expression of your walk with God.

Now a question. Is government inherently good or evil?

It is neither.

Weeds, Wheat and Fields

Jesus explained things very simply. He did this through the use of metaphors, stories and illustrations.

You and I have much to learn from the Master. Instead of trying to make ourselves sound smart through the use of multisyllabletoryian words and complexity of argument, we should aim for simplicity. When listening to someone drone on and on with a long-winded and incomprehensible explanation I usually think: *That dude doesn't really know what he is talking about. If he did, he would explain it in a way I could understand it.* Politicians use this technique to obscure an issue or avoid answering a question.

Another characteristic of Jesus' teaching was that he kept on topic.

Where was I going with this? Oh yeah. So I racked my brain trying to think of a simple way to describe the moral status of government. And then I gave up when I realized that Jesus had already explained the concept.

> He put another parable before them, saying, "The kingdom of heaven may be compared to a man who sowed good seed in his field, but while his men were

> sleeping, his enemy came and sowed weeds among the wheat and went away. So when the plants came up and bore grain, then the weeds appeared also. And the servants of the master of the house came and said to him, 'Master, did you not sow good seed in your field? How then does it have weeds?' He said to them, 'An enemy has done this.' So the servants said to him, 'Then do you want us to go and gather them?' But he said, 'No, lest in gathering the weeds you root up the wheat along with them. Let both grow together until the harvest, and at harvest time I will tell the reapers, "Gather the weeds first and bind them in bundles to be burned, but gather the wheat into my barn."'"
>
> Matthew 13:24-30

There is a "man" who sows wheat and an "enemy" who sows weeds. They sow in a "field," where the wheat and weeds grow together until the harvest time. Hopefully you understand what is going on here. (Hint: it is not about agriculture.) But in case you missed the point, Jesus interprets.

> The one who sows the good seed is the Son of Man. The **field is the world**, and the good seed is the sons of the kingdom. The weeds are the sons of the evil one, and the enemy who sowed them is the devil. The harvest is the end of the age, and the reapers are angels. Just as the weeds are gathered and burned with fire, so will it be at the end of the age. The Son of Man will send his angels, and they will gather out of his kingdom all causes of sin and all law-breakers, and throw them into the fiery furnace. In that place there will be weeping and gnashing of teeth. Then the righteous will shine like the sun in the kingdom of their Father.
>
> Matthew 13:37-43

Now view this parable from a kingdom perspective. Did you notice that there are three kingdoms in it? There is the kingdom of God (the man who sowed the good seed and the wheat), the kingdom of Satan (the enemy and the weeds), and the kingdom of the world (man's domain, the physical earth). I suppose the eternal kingdom is portrayed here too because God is accomplishing his sovereign purposes.

Here is the significant point for our discussion. The activity of BOTH spiritual kingdoms is occurring in the physical kingdom. The wheat and weeds grow together in the same field. The field does not make the wheat evil or the weeds good. Good and evil occur on the field but not because of the field. The field is morally neutral ground.

I suspect that you already view the physical earth this way. You do not think rocks and trees and mountains and seas are evil, do you? Even in the most horrific places, such as the Nazi death camps, you know that the devil-inspired evil that occurred there was not caused by the nature of the dirt but by the immoral actions of men.

Morality is not a physical property. It is a spiritual property.

Enough of dominion real estate. Now for the dominion institutions. Consider the office of president of the United States. Is the office itself either good or evil? No, it is not. But are the actions of the president either good or evil? Yes, they are. The office is the field. The wheat and weeds are growing on the field.

What is true for government is also true for the other dominion institutions. Politics are so often cynically mocked that we are tempted to consider it as different from the others. But it is not. Consider family, for example. Is the institution of family good or evil? The purpose of family as designed by God is good, of course. But both good and evil occur in families. It is also a battleground between the spiritual kingdoms.

If I were to wager on whether more evil occurred in government or family, I would put all of my chips on family. Think about what happened in only the first four chapters of Genesis (paraphrased):

> Eve to Adam: *Try this one, my dear.*
> Adam to God about Eve: *It's that she-devil's fault!*
> Cain to Abel: *I'll show you a better sacrifice, Brother!*

While government gets all the press, especially these days, and garners the more spectacular headlines, private sins within families are more devastating on the whole across the human race. Both evil and good occur in each of the ruler-rules-ruled institutions across man's dominion. Wheat and weeds are growing together on the field.

An Evil World?

There is one huge problem with your theory that man's domain is neutral. The Bible clearly describes the world as being evil.

You are half right. Sometimes it does. Sometimes it doesn't. Let me provide an example of each.

> And you were dead in the trespasses and sins in which you once walked, following the course of this **world**, following the prince of the power of the air, the spirit

> that is now at work in the sons of disobedience
> Ephesians 2:1-2

This is the usage you are referring to. Satan is clearly the ruler of the "world" in this sense. "World" is synonymous with his evil spiritual kingdom. But there is another meaning of the word.

> Of this you have heard before in the word of the truth, the gospel, which has come to you, as indeed in the whole **world** it is bearing fruit and increasing
> Colossians 1:5-6

"World," as used here, is not a reference to a spiritual association with the devil but to a physical location. It is about geography not morality. Where is the gospel "bearing fruit and increasing?" It is on the earth, man's domain.

It is nonsensical to interpret "world" in this passage as Satan's kingdom. The gospel does not "bear fruit" and "increase" in Satan's kingdom. The gospel drives out, defeats and replaces Satan's kingdom upon the battleground of the earth. You should be praying for this, as Jesus taught.

> Your **kingdom** come, your will be done, on **earth** as it is in **heaven**.
> Matthew 6:10

The context of a passage always reveals whether "world" is to be interpreted in the spiritual or physical sense.

Throughout Church history, unfortunately, some have interpreted "world" solely in the spiritually evil sense. If you make this error, you will consider the material realm to be inherently sinful and, as a result, be confused and conflicted about your earthly dominion responsibilities.

To assume that the material world is evil and the spiritual world is good is wrong twice. The material world is neither morally good nor evil. The spiritual world is both.

But if you want to confuse your theology with those beliefs, go ahead. At least you'll be in good company, as you will soon see.

So, man's domain—the material world, including the institutions that govern it—is neither good nor evil in the moral sense. It is merely the venue in which good and evil, right and wrong, occur in the great struggle between the spiritual kingdoms.

9 Kingdom Consolidation

Kingdom is one of the great themes in the Bible. It is far more extensive and detailed than I have described. I have only sketched the mere outlines of the current kingdoms and how they relate to your dominion responsibilities. But even my simple drawing may be more complex than you would like. *Why does this have to be so complicated?*

The four kingdoms are more assumed than explained throughout Scripture. They appear without background, summary or footnotes. This is especially true of the spiritual kingdoms, which are largely veiled in the Old Testament but suddenly the main attraction in the New.

But one thing should be very evident to every student of the Bible when it comes to kingdom. A better age is coming. God has a kingdom plan and all of history is moving toward its fulfillment. So let's move from what-is to what-will-be. What-will-be is anticipated throughout the Bible.

The Thunder Storm

You learn about the coming kingdom age largely in glimpses.

Most biblical text is about the people and places at the time of its writing. There is, of course, application for God's people of all ages. You learn about what you are to believe and do from God's dealings with others.

So here you are—the Bible scholar—reading carefully and paying attention to the historical context of a passage, and—FLASH!—suddenly there is a reference to something greater, to something future. It is like being in a thunder storm at night. You see nothing and then there is a brilliant light. It lasts only an instance, but it illuminates what is beyond.

God allows you a glimpse into the future.

FLASH—the curse of the serpent in the garden! FLASH—the covenant with Abraham that he will become a "great nation" and "all the families of the earth" will be blessed through him! FLASH—the promise to David that his kingdom and throne will be "established forever!"

There are foretastes of God's future kingdom plans. They flash suddenly, unexpectedly. But sometimes the thunder storm really gets intense, especially in portions of the prophetic books. *FLASH-BOOM! FLASH-BOOM!*

> For to us a child is born, to us a son is given; and the government shall be upon his shoulder, and his name shall be called Wonderful Counselor, Mighty God, Everlasting Father, Prince of Peace. Of the increase of his government and of peace there will be no end, on the throne of David and over his kingdom, to establish it and to uphold it with justice and with righteousness from this time forth and forevermore. The zeal of the LORD of hosts will do this.
>
> Isaiah 9:6-7

Future scenes are illuminated one after the other, often in vivid imagery.

The Book of Daniel has its share. Two of his visions are of particular interest to us. Why? Because these provide an abbreviated kingdom history. The first vision is of a great image constructed of various metals. The second is of the four beasts—a lion, a bear, a leopard and a hideous creature not described as an animal. These two visions may be viewed as one. The scenery is different but the plot is the same.

In each vision four kingdoms of the world are described. But our interest is the final kingdom. Here is how he describes it in the first vision:

> And in the days of those kings the God of heaven will set up **a kingdom** that shall never be destroyed, nor shall **the kingdom** be left to another people. It shall break in pieces all these kingdoms and bring them to an end, and it shall stand forever....
>
> Daniel 2:44

And in the second vision:

> And **the kingdom** and the dominion and the greatness of the kingdoms under the whole heaven shall be given to the people of the saints of the Most High; **his kingdom**

> shall be an **everlasting kingdom**, and all dominions shall serve and obey him. Here is the end of the matter.
>
> Daniel 7:27-28

There is something here that you cannot miss. There will be a final kingdom. It is God's kingdom and will be given to God's people, who serve and obey him. There is no longer an opposing spiritual kingdom or even a neutral human kingdom. Every trace of opposition will be destroyed and a single kingdom will exist forever.

That simplifies the kingdom picture quite a bit.

The vision of a unified future kingdom is consistent throughout the Scripture. I bring to your attention a few key verses from the New Testament.

> When the Son of Man comes in his glory, and all the angels with him, then he will sit on his glorious throne. Before him will be gathered all the nations, and he will separate people one from another as a shepherd separates the sheep from the goats. And he will place the sheep on his right, but the goats on the left. Then the King will say to those on his right, 'Come, you who are blessed by my Father, inherit the **kingdom prepared for you** from the foundation of the world.
>
> Matthew 25:31-34

> Then comes the end, when **he delivers the kingdom to God the Father** after destroying every rule and every authority and power. For he must reign until he has put all his enemies under his feet.
>
> I Corinthians 15:24-25

> In him [Jesus] we have redemption through his blood, the forgiveness of our trespasses, according to the riches of his grace, which he lavished upon us, in all wisdom and insight making known to us the mystery of his will, according to his **purpose**, which he set forth in Christ as a **plan** for the fullness of time, to **unite all things in him, things in heaven and things on earth**.
>
> Ephesians 1:7-10

> Then the seventh angel blew his trumpet, and there were loud voices in heaven, saying, "The **kingdom of the world** has become **the kingdom of our Lord and of his Christ**,

and he shall reign forever and ever."
Revelation 11:15

What should we call this future unified kingdom? Well…let's call it what Jesus calls it—the kingdom of God.

> "I have earnestly desired to eat this Passover with you before I suffer. For I tell you I will not eat it until it is **fulfilled in the kingdom of God**." And he took a cup, and when he had given thanks he said, "Take this, and divide it among yourselves. For I tell you that from now on I will not drink of the fruit of the vine **until the kingdom of God comes**."
>
> Luke 22:15-18

Hold it! I thought that you defined the "kingdom of God" as a spiritual kingdom. Now you say it will be the final unified kingdom?

Yes. It is presently a spiritual kingdom. In the future it will encompass both the spiritual and the material realms of creation, the unseen and the seen. Jesus will defeat the rebellion against God—the rebellion of both angels and men. All enemies of God will be imprisoned and suffer everlasting punishment.

In the next world there will be no more kingdom conflict. No more opposition to God. No more warfare between good and evil upon the earth. The redeemed will serve their King in full freedom and willing submission. All to his glory within the kingdom of God!

Pay Day

I will have to think about all of this kingdom stuff. What you are saying seems right, but I have not heard it explained so comprehensively before.

That's why I'm here.

One more question. What does the future kingdom have to do with my political involvement now?

Jesus answers that in the parable of the minas. Context: the master entrusts money to his servants. Two servants earn a good return and are commended.

> The first came before him, saying, 'Lord, your mina has made ten minas more.' And he said to him, 'Well done, good servant! Because you have been faithful in a very little, you shall have authority over ten cities.' And the second came, saying, 'Lord, your mina has made five

> minas.' And he said to him, 'And you are to be over five cities.'
>
> Luke 19:16-19

The biblical description of the coming kingdom age differs from the prevalent idea that the redeemed will become spirits floating through the ether singing an endless loop of the Hallelujah Chorus. Not exactly. The redeemed will be resurrected bodily and will serve their King on the new earth.

And how will the redeemed serve their King on the new earth? They will have government jobs. They will be ruling. They will have "authority over cities," as described in the parable.

And what determines the extent of their future responsibilities? Pay attention. It is faithfulness in fulfilling current responsibilities. The servants are given a little money to manage and, if they do well, they will gain much greater responsibilities. He who is faithful in a little will be set over much.

Having more ruling responsibility—brace yourself for this—is something you should desire. It is a motivation for greater godliness not less. Why? Because the greater your scope of ruling the more you can accomplish to glorify God.

So not only does an understanding of your role in the coming kingdom provide a hope that you can actually relate to, it greatly increases the importance of your work.

Think about it. If you consider your earthly responsibilities to be a temporary drudgery only to be discarded as "worldly chaff" when you enter heaven, then why would you work hard at them? But if you see your work as the basis for future blessing—your job performance evaluation from Jesus—what you do becomes very important and consequential. All of your dominion responsibilities take on an eternal significance.

Now back to the minas. This parable in particular promises greater political responsibility. "Authority over cities" means ruling over cities. Ruling over cities means governing them. And governing means that politics are involved.

In case you think that I have made too much out of a parable, the theme of future ruling responsibilities is consistent scriptural theme. You find it in many places, such as here:

> And I saw no temple in the city, for its temple is the Lord God the Almighty and the Lamb. And the city has no need of sun or moon to shine on it, for the glory of God gives it light, and its lamp is the Lamb. By its light will the

> **nations** walk, and the **kings of the earth** will bring their glory into it....
>
> Revelation 21:22-24

In the coming kingdom of God there will be nations and kings, that is human government. But unlike now, all will completely serve and honor the King of kings and Lord of lords.

You may have a difficult time imagining politics without the corruption of sin. I do. But so it shall be. No scheming, conniving and deceiving. No character assassination. No destructive polarization. Just good governance.

A Final Word About Kingdom

There is nothing more crucial to a biblical perspective than understanding its kingdom teaching. It is the continuing narrative that begins in Genesis and concludes in Revelation. It is the context for your identity in Christ. And it explains your role in this world and the next.

Focusing only on kingdom's spiritual aspects often leads to escape from or confusion about the material world and its dominion responsibilities. Focusing only on kingdom's material aspects obscures the spiritual realities behind all that is seen. Hold on to both for the right balance of practice and meaning.

10 Regarding the Church

Where does the church fit into all of this kingdom stuff?
Good question.
So answer it.
Before you can understand the relationship of the church to the kingdoms, you must understand the church. What exactly is the church?

The Institutional Church

Once again distinctions are required. There are two ways in which the word "church" is used in the New Testament. The great majority of references are to a gathering of Christians for teaching, worship, community and outreach. This is the visible church, the physical church, the institutional church.

The institutional aspect is that a church has rulers, rules and the ruled. The rulers are the elders and whatever denominational hierarchy there may be. The rules are the standards of conduct and doctrinal boundaries. The ruled are the members of the congregation—the "sheep" in the somewhat unflattering biblical lingo.

Like family, employment and government, the rulers are accountable for ruling justly and the ruled are accountable for obeying the rulers when they do.

But you should not assume that everyone in the institutional church is a Christian. Stepping into a church building no more makes you a Christian than stepping into a barn makes you a cow. Or better yet, to borrow from Jesus' analogy, there are usually some weeds mixed in with the wheat…even in a church.

The Apostle John refers to some who denied the most basic tenet of Christianity, that Jesus is the Christ.

> They went out from us, but they were not of us; for if they had been of us, they would have continued with us. But they went out, that it might become plain that they all are not of us.
>
> I John 2:19

Some who had been in church "went out from us." The weeds were removed. Unfortunately, sometimes the weeds creep into positions of influence and a church becomes overgrown with them. Jesus warns the seven churches in the book of Revelation to remain faithful to him…or else.

> Remember therefore from where you have fallen; repent, and do the works you did at first. If not, I will come to you and remove your lampstand from its place, unless you repent.
>
> Revelation 2:5

This is no idle threat. The history of Christianity is littered with apostate churches. They retain the symbols of Christianity but reject the faith. So the lights go out—first spiritually and eventually physically.

Now it should be evident that the institutional church is not located on hallowed ground. It is located on neutral ground—just like the dominion institutions. Spiritual warfare is as intense inside the visible church as it is outside. If you doubt this, just read through the Epistles and see all of the struggles of the early Christians.

Now a question. Does the institutional church replace the dominion institutions? Does the authority of your church leadership supersede the authority of family, employment and government rulers? Some have said that they do. There are many examples in history…and even today.

But I think not. Why? Because the consistent and repeated instruction in the New Testament is to support the dominion institutions not supplant them. Christians are commanded to submit to all authorities.

The Universal Church

The second way in which the word "church" is used in the New Testament is in reference to all true Christians. This is the invisible church, the spiritual church, the universal church. To use two biblical metaphors, this is the body and bride of Christ.

The spiritual nature of the universal church is seen in this passage.

> ...so that through the **church** the manifold wisdom of God might now be made known to the rulers and authorities in the heavenly places.
>
> Ephesian 3:10

And in this one.

> And he [Jesus] is the head of the body, the **church**.
>
> Colossians 1:18

So there are these two uses of "church" in the New Testament. The one is physical and institutional, the other is spiritual and universal.

* * *

Okay. I get it. But I am interested in the interaction between the institutional church and the institution of government. No...that sounds too abstract. I'll try again. Should my church be involved in politics?

11 Kingdom Confusion

Let's look at some historical examples of church-government relations. To best explain these, I will describe them as kingdom models, theologies of how physical and spiritual realities interact, which is what they are. As you study them—or at least my crude depiction of them—you will notice that they differ significantly from mine, as well as from each other.

In each case, count the number of kingdoms. How many are there? Also, pay attention to what is meant by "church." Is it the institutional church, the universal church, or a combination or both? The blurring of these biblical distinctions ends in confusion about political involvement, as well as all other earthly responsibilities.

The Hands of God

Martin Luther (1483-1546), the great Protestant Reformer, described God as ruling the world with his right and left hands. His hands are his "Two Kingdoms," his governments. His right hand is the heavenly kingdom (the universal Church). His left hand is the worldly kingdom. The right is spiritual and internal. The left is physical and external. Since the institutional church (the visible church) is physical, like government, Luther places both of them in the left hand of God. Here is how I draw this.

THE KINGDOM OF THE WORLD

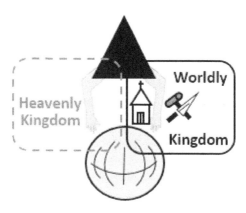

I like Luther. He is my type of guy...a hero of mine, in fact. And I like his analogy of the two hands of God. It is vivid, simple to understand, and supports the biblical commands to obey government rulers. This was the model that shaped my political perspective for many years.

Ideas have consequences, as they say. What are the consequences of a model emphasizing God's rule? To begin with, government must be inherently good. To obey government is to obey God. To disobey government is to disobey God.

But the most striking outworking of Luther's concept has been the state church. As I mentioned, he placed the visible church in the worldly kingdom and the invisible Church in the heavenly kingdom. Since the state and the visible church are both in the worldly kingdom, it follows that there should be a union between the two. That is what happened in the Lutheran and Reformed countries.

Although there were theoretical boundaries for each institution in this church-state alliance, in practice the church became subjugated to the state, in effect a department of the government. While some may argue in favor of this, from my perspective it has not benefited the churches. Just consider, for example, the vitality of the state churches in Europe today.

But there certainly was a practical reason for state churches, in the early days at least. Without the protection of the local government rulers, the Protestants would have ended up on Roman Catholic bonfires. Given that choice, I might have politicked for a church-state union myself.

The Swords of God

Speaking of Roman Catholics, two hundred years before the Reformation church-state relations were defined in the "Two Sword" doctrine. The church wields a spiritual sword and the state wields a temporal sword on behalf of the church. The temporal authority is subject to the spiritual authority.

There is only one kingdom in this construct. It is the Roman Catholic Church. Who is the ruler of this kingdom that controls government? Let's trace the authority from the top down. God rules over his kingdom—the Roman Catholic Church. The Pope is God's ruling representative on earth. The state exercises government power in support of the Pope.

Both the Lutheran and Catholic models emphasize God's rule. God rules the world directly through human rulers, whether they be Pope or prince. So although differing on details, both sides of the Reformation struggle agreed on this.

The City of Man

Another kingdom model stands in stark contrast to these. Instead of seeing government as the rule of God, it is seen as the rule of the devil. Admittedly, this perspective is very tempting, especially in times of frustration with politics.

I will exhume this perspective from another historical voice—a great Church Father, highly respected by both Catholics and Protestants. And he wrote about it in one of the most influential works of Christian theology.

Do you know who said that "government is a necessary evil?" This is often attributed to Augustine of Hippo (354-430). But, as far as I can tell, he never wrote these words. They are found in the second paragraph of Thomas Paine's *Common Sense*.

THE KINGDOM OF THE WORLD

> Society in every state is a blessing, but **government**, even in its best state, **is** but **a necessary evil**; in its worst state an intolerable one.

Paine (1737-1809) was political activist and theorist, a revolutionary and a philosopher. He was not a father of the church but a father of the American Revolution. *Common Sense* is arguably the most popular and influential American political pamphlet ever published. It was even read aloud in taverns, as I am sure this book will be. But I begin to drift again.

While the origin of the phrase "government is a necessary evil" may not have been coined by Augustine, it correctly summarizes his perspective on the subject, which explains the attribution error.

Consider the two modifying words "necessary" and "evil." That government is necessary is commonly agreed upon, as it should be, although Augustine argues that it was only necessary after sin, while I make a case that is was inherent in the Dominion Mandate, which was given before man's sin. But this may be a bit of theological hair splitting with little practical implication. Whether or not government is evil is a much more significant question.

Augustine wrote about the relationship of the Christian to society most thoroughly in *The City of God*. He divided mankind into two groups. There is the City of Man (also referred to as the city of this world, the earthly city, and the city of the devil) and the City of God. Augustine summarized the difference here:

> And certainly this is the great difference which distinguishes the two cities of which we speak, the one being the society of the godly men, the other of the ungodly, each associated with the angels that adhere to their party, and the one guided and fashioned by love of self, the other by love of God.[6]

Every person is a citizen of one city or the other—the redeemed in the City of God; the rebels in the City of man. Each city is associated with good or evil spiritual beings, the angels and the demons. Each city is ruled by a king—the one by Jesus, the other by the devil[7].

---

[6] *City of God*, XIV:13.
[7] *City of God*, XIV:13, XVII:20 and XVIII:41.

What is the biblical basis for Augustine's two cities? The City of God metaphor is drawn from the book of Hebrews,[8] although there is no such direct reference to the City of man.

This, of course, is the very briefest of summaries. Augustine expounds on the two cities in over 800 dense pages. He sometimes even apologizes at the end of a section for cutting it short when there is so much more to say. The man was not guilty of conciseness.

To return to the critical point, Augustine places government in the City of Man—Satan's city. Government is the rule of the devil.

Pendulums and Tides

Just so the record is clear, I am not saying that all Lutherans or Catholics or Augustinians still hold to these positions. Some may. Some may have moved on. Theologies tend to morph in response to the commotion of the day. This is especially true in the area of politics. If the government is persecuting you, you are tempted to see it as the scourge of the devil. If the government is favorable toward you, surely it must be the hand of God.

Evangelicals tend to swing back and forth on this pendulum every so many years or so to make sure we cover both extremes. It is easy to be swept along in the tide of the latest political events.

These are general reasons for theological inconsistency in political involvement. In addition, there are specific difficulties that come with government being within either the kingdom of God or the kingdom of Satan.

---

[8] See Hebrews 11:10, 11:16, 12:22-24 and 13:14.

THE KINGDOM OF THE WORLD

Luther's Dilemma

Let us proceed to an event in the life of Martin Luther that illustrates his challenge. The event was the Diet of Worms (1521). This was not some all-natural high-protein craze but a heresy trial called by the emperor to force Luther to affirm or recant his writings.

At this point in his career Luther had rejected the religious authority of the Roman Catholic Church, but he accepted the political authority of the Holy Roman Empire, as expressed here:

> You ask me what I shall do if I am called by the emperor. I will go even if I am too sick to stand on my feet. If Caesar calls me, God calls me.[9]

"If Caesar calls me, God calls me." Luther equated a summons from the government ruler as a summons from God. This is consistent with his government-is-the-left-hand-of-God theology. And this clear and easy to follow political position worked well…until the emperor ruled against Luther in the Edict of Worms. Here are a few excerpts so that you can get the gist of it:

> …This devil [Luther] in the habit of a monk has brought together ancient errors into one stinking puddle and has invented new ones. …He lives the life of a beast. …He does more harm to the civil than the ecclesiastical power. …no one is to harbor him. His followers also are to be condemned. His books are to be eradicated from the memory of man.[10]

I must admit that I enjoy the clarity of debate that occurred during Reformation days. Lawyers and English majors were not required to determine the precise meaning of the words. Everyone could pretty much understand what was being said right off the bat.

Fortunately for the Reformation, Luther disobeyed the emperor. So did the German princes that hid and protected the renegade monk. But the problem here is that if you really think that obeying government is obeying God, then you must come to the conclusion that disobeying government is disobeying God.

How did Luther justify disobeying the emperor? I don't know for sure.

---

[9] Roland H. Bainton, *Here I Stand: A Life of Martin Luther* (New York: Abingdon-Cokesbury Press, 1950), 174.
[10] Ibid., 189.

Perhaps the complexities of the political situation offered him a way out. The German princes owed allegiance to the emperor. The emperor owed justice to the princes. Did the princes disobey God by defying the emperor? Or was the emperor's authority illegitimate because he lacked the support of the princes? You can flip that coin either way. In any case, Luther did not alter his political theology.

Competing claims of government authority always raise a difficult question. *Whose side is God on?* Or the more spiritually correct: *Who is on God's side?* This is unavoidable. Because history is often told as the struggle for government power, competing claims to governmental authority is a common occurrence. And if you believe that government rule is God's rule, then the ultimate issue is determining who exactly represents God.

Now I shall let my friend Martin rest in peace. On to Augustine.

Serving Satan

The burden that comes with the two-cities theology is just the opposite of the two-hands and two-swords theologies. The difficulty is not to explain why you should disobey God but why you should support the devil. To me, this is the greater challenge.

Augustine was clever enough to provide an argument that justifies it. Basically he said that there is common cause between the City of God and the City of Man, a place for cooperation between adversaries. What is the common cause? It is civil order. It is because civil order is necessary that government—evil though it may be—is necessary.

While both the City of God and the City of Man seek civil order, they do so for different reasons. Unbelievers strive to maintain civil order for selfish reasons, such as to maintain the ruler's power or achieve greater prosperity. Christians support civil order out of love for God and neighbor. Different desires but a shared outcome. In other words, it is okay to serve the devil's kingdom if your motives are pure. You can obey both God and Satan.

But this seems suspect, whether it is necessary or not.

> Abstain from every form of evil.
> I Thessalonians 5:22

I understand your point, but what about the Gospel account of Satan offering the kingdoms of the world to Jesus? Doesn't that prove that the devil owns the nations?

THE KINGDOM OF THE WORLD

The Devil's Bargain

Let's look at that passage.

> Again, the devil took him [Jesus] to a very high mountain and showed him all the kingdoms of the world and their glory. And he said to him, "All these I will give you, if you will fall down and worship me."
>
> Matthew 4:8-9

Interpret the text.

I think it means that Satan rules over the nations—the kingdoms of the world—like Augustine said. He offers to give them to Jesus, which means that they must be his to give.

Satan is the "father of lies," you know.

Maybe he is telling the truth here. Jesus did not correct him.

Jesus refused to worship him, which was Satan's main objective, and then dismissed him. He did not address Satan's claim to the kingdoms of the world one way or the other.

> Then Jesus said to him, "Be gone, Satan! For it is written,
> "'You shall worship the Lord your God and him only shall you serve.'"
>
> Matthew 4:10

So do not make an assumption based upon something Jesus did not say. This is an argument from silence, which is always a weak foundation. It is best to build theology upon a theme of Scripture—something that is clearly taught throughout the Bible.

Political Pressures

Each of the three kingdom theologies I briefly describe above were formed in the political currents of their day.

Luther's two-hands was birthed in the violent religious and social turmoil of the Reformation period. It was the rationale for the church-state union that protected the Protestants. The Roman Catholic two-swords sought to undergird the rule of church over state in the tug-of-war for power that had been occurring since the Middle Ages. And Augustine's two-cities defended Christians against the charge of weakening the Roman state.

I am, admittedly, painting with a broad brush. The point is that politics have shaped theology throughout history. And this continues. You are not above political influences. Nobody is. I just want you to recognize them.

Good or Evil?

The most important observation about these theologies is that the institution of government is considered to be either inherently good or inherently evil. Government is good in two-hands and two-swords because it is the rule of God. Government is evil in two-cities because it is the rule of Satan.

Let me illustrate this by returning to the dominion portion of my clever little illustration.

By emphasizing the rule of God, as in two-hands and two-swords, the practical effect, intentionally or otherwise, results in downplaying man's ruling responsibility, especially the evil he may do. The little crown might as well not exist.

When government is seen as the rule of Satan, as in two-cities, man's responsibility is again ignored, especially the good he may do. In this case, the little crown has not disappeared. The devil is wearing it.

THE KINGDOM OF THE WORLD

Here's the thing. You do not have to choose whether the institution of government is good or evil. That is a false dilemma, a false choice. There is the third option. Government is neutral like the physical earth and every other institution through which man rules over it.

* * *

I may or may not have persuaded you that my kingdom model most accurately reflects biblical teaching. You may or may not agree that the church, as an institution, is neutral ground. But you cannot deny that your understanding of the kingdoms and their relationship to the church lays the foundation for your politics, as well as for all other involvement in the world.

12 Where is the Church?

The institutional church is essential to the historical kingdom models I have described. In fact, the purpose of those models is largely to explain the relationship between church and state.

Now look again at my model. Do you notice anything missing?

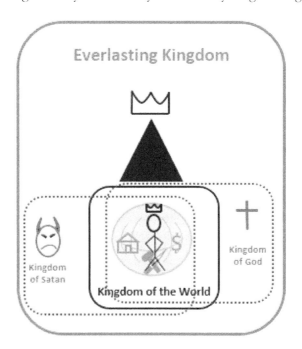

I have not included the institutional church. Why? Because it is not a spiritual or physical kingdom. And it is not a dominion institution through which man rules the earth. So what is a church? It is an organized assembly of those who profess faith in Jesus and are gathered together in Christian community in order to teach, encourage, exhort, and, if necessary, discipline one another to live in obedience to God.

From a kingdom perspective, a church is to express the reality of the kingdom of God in the kingdom of the world. "Your kingdom come, your will be done, on earth as it is in heaven."

So then, a church is a physical institution with a spiritual purpose.

> Obey your leaders and submit to them, for they are keeping watch over your **souls**, as those who will have to give an account.
> Hebrews 13:17

The rulers of a church—the elders and any denominational hierarchy—have a "soul" purpose. They are to be "keeping watch over your souls." They are the shepherds of the sheep.

So you are saying that the church…my church…should not be involved in politics. You are a separation-of-church-and-state guy.

I'll answer that by describing the proper and improper separation of church and state.

Church and state should be institutionally separate. Rulers of the state should not be the rulers of a church and vice versa. Different rulers with different rules. Government is responsible for the civil order. A church is responsible for order within the congregation.

A church, however, should not be influentially separate from the politics that shape the state. In order to be faithful to its God-given charter, a church must teach the Bible. All of it. As I hope you agree by now, the Bible has much to say about politics. And teaching the Bible involves not only interpreting the text but applying the text to the issues of the day.

The political influence a church exerts on its members is no different from the influence it exerts regarding good or evil in the other dominion institutions of family and employment. Should a church teach that a husband is required to love his wife, that a wife must respect her husband, and that children are obligated to obey their parents? Should a church teach that a boss is to treat his employees with dignity and that the employees should work hard for the boss? Of course. And this teaching should not only repeat the biblical commands but show how they are to be practiced.

Having said that, a Christian does not exercise his political responsibilities (or other dominion responsibilities) as the member of a church. He exercises his political responsibilities as a citizen—one who exhibits the kingdom of God on earth, which is what a church should equip him to do.

WHERE IS THE CHURCH?

Wife Beaters and Tax Cheaters

Take the case of a man beating his wife. Should this be a concern for the elders of his church? Yes. Not because the church replaces or usurps family authority, but because the man's actions dishonor Christ and discredit the people of God. The man is responsible before God for his sin. The church leadership is responsible before God to rebuke him and to put him out of the church if he refuses to repent.

Furthermore, the man's wife-beating behavior brings his faith into question. I am not saying that he has lost his faith but that he may not have it. Repentance is an evidence of faith. Rebellion is an indication that it does not exist. Or, more simply, you will know a tree by its fruit, as Jesus said.

A church disciplines a person for the sake of his soul. The government punishes him to maintain order in society.

The government should not be concerned about the man's faith. But it should be concerned about stopping his physical abuse of his wife, which threatens the social order. That is the purpose of cops, judges and jails.

Now for a political example. Suppose a man cheats on his taxes. This would normally be a private sin unknown in the church. Suppose, though, that he openly brags about it. He even encourages others in the church to do it. And he is persuasive. *The government is immoral. Starve the beast! And give that money to the church instead.*

What is the responsibility of the elders? Is it to put the man in charge of the next capital campaign? Tempting...but no. The elders should rebuke him and, if that fails to change his behavior, then discipline him. But it is not the role of the church to prosecute and punish the man for breaking the law. That is the government's job.

This is an easy example because the Scripture teaches you in clear and direct commands to pay your taxes. But some situations are not always so clean cut.

Yeah, like when the government requires me to do something that is actually immoral. What do I do then?

Yes, that happens—not because the institution is immoral but because the particular rulers and rules may be. Patience, my friend. We are almost to the next section, where I will address this. My point here is that the church has a different institutional role than the dominion institutions.

Judge One Another

Another question. Where are the institutional boundaries between church and state? Where should they be? You may have noticed that these borders vary from nation to nation. And even within a nation they often shift around. While the Bible does not provide a one-size-fits-all template, the Apostle Paul has provided some useful guidelines that will help you sort this out.

In his letter to the Romans, Paul describes the individual's responsibility to submit to the state. But in his first letter to the Corinthians, his instruction is to the institutional church to discipline the sinful behavior of its members.

Let's take a peek.

> I wrote to you in my letter not to associate with sexually immoral people—not at all meaning the sexually immoral of this world, or the greedy and swindlers, or idolaters, since then you would need to go out of the world. But now I am writing to you not to associate with anyone who bears the name of brother if he is guilty of sexual immorality or greed, or is an idolater, reviler, drunkard, or swindler—not even to eat with such a one. For what have I to do with judging outsiders? Is it not those inside the church whom you are to judge? God judges those outside. "Purge the evil person from among you."
>
> I Corinthians 5:9-13

The passage is about judgement. This is not merely disapproving of some behavior. It includes an official action against rule breakers.

Paul describes who is and who is not to be judged by a church. Brothers, who are insiders, are to be judged. Outsiders are not.

Excommunication is a church's judgement, which is excluding a person from a body of believers. But a church does not have the authority to remove a person from the church who is not in the church. I make this sound silly so that you won't miss the point. Paul limits a church's judgement to those within the church.

For everyone else, "God judges those outside."

How does he do that?

God judges individuals directly. If you violate the great commands, there will be consequences both now and on the last day. But he also exercises judgement through institutions. Excommunication is his judgement by a church. Civil punishment is his judgement by the state.

Now review Paul's laundry list of sinners in the passage above. This is illustrative not comprehensive.

Sexual Immoral
Greedy
Swindler

WHERE IS THE CHURCH?

> Idolater
> Reviler
> Drunkard

Does God directly judge these sinners? Yes. Should a church judge these sinners? Yes, in some cases. Should. the government judge these sinners? Yes, again in some cases.

Hold on! Explain that.

Take greed, for example. Church elders should not excommunicate Junior for scarfing down the last three donuts on the refreshment tray. Neither should the police chief dispatch a squad car to arrest the boy. His behavior should be addressed by another institution—the family.

Furthermore, all sins cannot be judged by human institutions. Only God is able to discern Junior's greedy heart. A church errs when it judges desires or motivations instead of actions. The same goes for the state.

But a church should judge greedy behavior, such as when a member is embezzling money from his employer. His actions dishonor Christ and discredit the church. The local magistrate should also press charges but for a different reason. Embezzlement is a violation of the civil law. Is this double jeopardy? No, it is not. Church and state have separate rulers and rules, separate jurisdictions, although one may be subject to both.

A church should judge a member for drunkenness. A state may have no law against getting drunk, per se, but should have laws about this condition when it threatens the public order, such as drunk driving or unruly behavior.

I could go on and on with examples from each of the sins above…but I won't. I trust that you grasp the difference between church and state judgements.

Judge Among Yourselves

Paul then flips his argument. While a church should not judge outsiders, the state should not be called upon to resolve disputes between insiders.

> When one of you has a grievance against another, does he dare go to law before the unrighteous instead of the saints? Or do you not know that the saints will judge the world? And if the world is to be judged by you, are you incompetent to try trivial cases? Do you not know that we are to judge angels? How much more, then, matters pertaining to this life! So if you have such cases, why do you lay them before those who have no standing in the church? I say this to your shame. Can it be that there is

> no one among you wise enough to settle a dispute between the brothers, but brother goes to law against brother, and that before unbelievers? To have lawsuits at all with one another is already a defeat for you. Why not rather suffer wrong? Why not rather be defrauded? But you yourselves wrong and defraud—even your own brothers!
>
> I Corinthians 6:1-8

Context first. What is at issue here? "When one of you has a grievance against another." In other words, this is a dispute between believers. It is not an offense against the state, a criminal violation. This is a civil suit.

Does the government have authority under God to judge these type of cases? Yes, it does. Why? Because it is necessary for social order. It provides an orderly, impartial and nonviolent way to achieve justice and resolve conflicts between citizens.

Why then does Paul rebuke the Corinthian Christians from seeking state resolution of their conflicts with each other? Because they should have been able to resolve such matters themselves. And if they could not, they should have asked for help from within the church.

I was involved in such a case years ago. Two members of our church had reached an impasse. One was a contractor who had built a house for the other. The dispute was over change orders to the contract and their cost. Both members realized that it would bring shame on the church and themselves if they took this issue to court. So they voluntarily agreed to submit to an arbitration panel on which I served. As it turned out, both sides had valid points and neither side was completely satisfied by our ruling. But Jesus is honored when Christians are able to settle an issue between themselves without government intervention.

* * *

So…where are you going to put the little church symbol in your kingdom model?
   I'm not putting it in.
Why not?
   It does not belong. But if this bothers you, take a pencil and draw it wherever you wish.

Living in the Kingdom
Part II

In Part One I constructed a theology of politics. I built this upon the broad and clear teaching of Scripture. That is, I attempted to state the obvious. However, all serious biblical theologians lay claim to this approach. And I have picked a fight with some of the most serious and most renown.

So…how do you know who is right?

Before I answer that, understand the nature of theology. It is a system of logic. You begin with a premise—an assumption or presupposition—and draw one or more conclusions from it. I am not criticizing this. It is the way we have been created to think about things.

The problem usually enters not with the conclusions but with the premises, which sometimes widely miss the mark but often are only incomplete. The statement may be half true. Or three-quarters. To put this more bluntly, your logic is usually right but the premise that led you there may be wrong.

So how do you know?

I suggest reading the Bible. All of it. Repeatedly. Nothing supports good interpretation like the flow of context. And as you are carried along by the words, you begin to see the currents, the larger themes, of Scripture.

The Bible, interestingly, teaches in two ways—by instruction and illustration, by theology and biography, by precept and practice. It is not enough to just intellectually acknowledge the words. Living them is also necessary. And those that live the words faithfully show the rest of us how to do it. They are our examples and we should follow them.

To that end, I will observe a few of the faithful. Most of the ones I have selected are biblical men and women of good character. The last two lived more recently—within the last couple of hundred years or so—and are also respectable.

As you read about them, ask yourself some questions. Do they exercise dominion ruling responsibilities in the various circumstances in which they find themselves? And in these situations, is government portrayed as neutral ground? That is, do you see both good and evil actions occurring in politics, depending upon the moral actions of the men and women? And behind these outworkings in the kingdom of the world, do you sense the spiritual influences of the kingdom of God and the opposing kingdom of Satan, as well as the sovereignty of God ruling over all in his everlasting kingdom? Are there unseen forces at work as well as what is seen?

Take a look.

13 Joseph

Genesis 37-47
Circa 19th Century BC

Horatio Alger (1832-99) was an American author known for his rags-to-riches stories. I have only read two of his books. I enjoyed them but feel no need to read others. They are all pretty much the same. An impoverished boy in difficult circumstances betters his position through hard work, determination and honesty.

That is the storyline of Joseph. *Slave becomes prime minister of Egypt through hard work, determination and honesty.* But our interest is not in his inspiring Horatio Alger-like journey to improved social status. Our interest is in his politics. And on this topic there is much to learn.

Sibling Rivalry

You should be familiar with Joseph's biography. He was the son of Jacob and Rachel. The favorite son of the favorite wife. In case his brothers missed the focus of their father's affections, Jacob made Joseph a special coat, a coat of many colors. This, needless to say, did not endear them to Joseph. They hated him.

The familial bonds were further frayed when Joseph dreamed two dreams. In the first, his brothers' sheaves of grain bowed down to Joseph's sheaves. Predictable results: they hated him even more. In the second dream, the sun, the moon, and eleven stars—his family—bowed down to him. Even the indulgent Jacob thought that this was going a bit too far.

Why didn't his family just laugh off his dreams? *Hah! You shouldn't have eaten that fifth slice of pizza last night.* They did not laugh them off because they knew that God communicated through dreams. And the meaning of this dream was very clear.

> Are you indeed to reign over us? Or are you indeed to rule over us?
>
> Genesis 37:8

Suddenly a story of tension within the institution of family expands into the institution of government. That this young whippersnapper should exercise government authority over the brothers would be the ultimate humiliation for them. So they decided to do something about it—a pre-emptive political assassination.

The opportunity came when Jacob sent Joseph to check up on his brothers. (For the record, Joseph had a history of giving his father a "bad report" on his brothers.) When they saw him coming, they plotted. Death was the straightforward solution to stop both his tattling and his ruling over them. Their logic was sound.

But this was surely evil politics. What crime had he committed? None. Tattling and dreaming are not crimes. But even if they were, the brothers had no authority to execute Joseph.

Fortunately, they did not carry out this scheme—fortunate for Joseph but also for us in our exploration of politics. As the eldest, Reuben knew that he would have to explain things to their father, and that their contrived he-was-killed-by-an-animal fiction would be hard to sell. So he convinced them to throw Joseph into a pit instead.

Reuben intended to rescue him, but while he was away a caravan of Ishmaelites just happened to be passing by. The brothers—minus Reuben—smelled cash and sold Joseph to them for twenty shekels of silver. In addition to gaining a tidy sum, this had the benefit of not burdening their consciences with murder.

Although slavery was the common practice of the day, the brothers had neither just cause nor right to kidnap and sell Joseph. The Ishmaelites were businessmen risking an investment in order to gain a profit. If there was any fault on their side, it may have been that they were lax in validating Joseph's slave status. But paperwork is often pencil-whipped in these out-of-the-way places.

In any case, the Ishmaelite caravan just happened to be going to Egypt. There they sold Joseph to Potiphar.

House Slave

Let us now try to view things from Joseph's perspective.

He was trapped in a system in which there seemed to be no way out. Where could he file an appeal? Who would help him? Answers: Nowhere and no one. Slaves had little legal recourse. That was one of the downsides of being a slave. No Egyptian legal aid society for Joseph. So what could he do?

Nothing. He was powerless.

Ah, there you are. I thought you were dozing through this part. Actually...a person is never completely powerless politically. The rulers may possess the civil authority and power, but the ruled determine how they will respond, which, as I have pointed out, is also a political act.

Joseph could have responded to the injustice of his situation by refusing to comply. *I will not legitimize this government system by fulfilling my duties as a slave!* Or by going on a hunger strike. *Think of the moral indignation I will provoke!* Or by escaping. *I can pass myself off as an Egyptian if I hold my nose up in the air.* Or by leading a slave rebellion. *Follow me you oppressed, you downtrodden, you wretched refuse!*

Joseph took none of these paths. Instead he complied. No, that is not the right word. He *excelled*. He excelled within the system as it was. How do I know that?

> The LORD was with Joseph, and he became a successful man, and he was in the house of his Egyptian master. His master saw that the LORD was with him and that the LORD caused all that he did to succeed in his hands. So Joseph found favor in his sight and attended him, and he made him overseer of his house and put him in charge of all that he had.
>
> Genesis 39:2-4

This inspired history leaves no room for an interpretation that Joseph was in any way compromising his integrity by sinning against God. Joseph succeeded in slavehood because God was with him. Why was God with him? Because Joseph was acting righteously in these difficult circumstances.

A Turn for the Worse

But soon—just like in a Horatio Alger story—there was more trouble. Woman trouble, in this case. Potiphar's wife desired Joseph. When he resisted her advances, she became spiteful and accused him of attempted rape. Potiphar, having legal authority over his slave, threw Joseph into prison.

This had to be...ah...discouraging to Joseph. Slavery was bad enough. Now prison! The system was entirely against him. That alone would tend to rankle a person. What made matters worse was that Joseph was not appreciated in the least for doing everything right.

At this point we would forgive Joseph for, perhaps, becoming a little moody. Who wouldn't be? But the man's response is again not what is expected.

> But the LORD was with Joseph and showed him steadfast love and gave him favor in the sight of the keeper of the prison. And the keeper of the prison put Joseph in charge of all the prisoners who were in the prison. Whatever was done there, he was the one who did it. The keeper of the prison paid no attention to anything that was in Joseph's charge, because the LORD was with him. And whatever he did, the LORD made it succeed.
> Genesis 39:21-23

There is no need for me to again describe the alternate options—prison break, etc. Joseph once more accepted his circumstances and honored God in them.

Then Pharaoh's cupbearer and baker showed up. You know the story. They dreamed dreams. Joseph interpreted the dreams. Things turn out well for the cupbearer but not so much for the baker.

It is here that the story begins to get interesting for us. After Joseph gives the cupbearer a favorable interpretation, he says this to him:

> Only remember me, when it is well with you, and please do me the kindness to mention me to Pharaoh, and so get me out of this house. For I was indeed stolen out of the land of the Hebrews, and here also I have done nothing that they should put me into the pit.
> Genesis 40:14-15

Joseph appeals to the very head of government! In a significant breech of protocol, he goes straight to the top, to Pharaoh. In legal terms, this would be called a "long shot." For a slave like Joseph this was perhaps the only shot. The chance of success seems…well…doubtful.

Probabilities aside, note the substance of Joseph's appeal. He is asking for justice from Pharaoh not mercy. He says that he was "stolen" and has done "nothing" wrong. Why did God give Pharaoh the authority to rule? In order to provide justice. Joseph knew his theology and Pharaoh's responsibility.

There is something else important here. I have said that Joseph was willing to "accept" his circumstances. This is in the same sense that the Apostle Paul meant when he wrote that he had learned to be content in every situation.[11] But being content did not mean that Paul did not try to change a situation for the better if he had opportunity. And opportunity often involved government, as it did for Joseph.

Joseph wanted to influence government. The problem was that the cupbearer forgot all about Joseph.

A Turn for the Better

Then it just so happened that Pharaoh had some dreams. Seven fat cows and seven ugly, thin ones. Seven plump ears of grain and seven thin, blighted ones. Who could interpret this? The cupbearer finally remembered Joseph and he was hastily tidied up and brought before Pharaoh.

This is what he said:

> Pharaoh, the dreams reveal that your government is in a heap of trouble. Good luck with trying to hold things together through the seven lean years. But let me get to the heart of the matter. You need to serve the One True God, which will require reinventing this pagan government from top to bottom. Anything less is like commanding that bricks be made without straw. And who would be stupid enough to do that?

Okay, I made up all of that, although the bricks-without-straw comment might have been filed away in the archives for later use.

Now to what really happened. Joseph interpreted the dreams. But he does not stop there. This is significant. He goes on to outline a government program to deal with the coming famine.

> Now therefore let Pharaoh select a discerning and wise man, and set him over the land of Egypt. Let Pharaoh proceed to appoint overseers over the land and take one-fifth of the produce of the land of Egypt during the seven plentiful years. And let them gather all the food of these good years that are coming and store up grain under the authority of Pharaoh for food in the cities, and let them keep it. That food shall be a reserve for the land against the seven years of famine that are to occur in the land of Egypt, so that the land may not perish through the famine.
>
> Genesis 41:33-36

---

[11] See Philippians 4:11.

Notice how Joseph begins. He shrewdly suggests that "Pharaoh select a discerning and wise man." Who might that be? The Egyptian intelligentsia that could not interpret a simple dream? Those dunderheads? Nope. Pharaoh makes Joseph his "number one" and gives him authority over all of Egypt.

Joseph took the initiative at every opportunity God gave him. The dreams of his youth that he would rule gave him the confidence for political action not inaction. He was not passive. *Whatever will be, will be.* No.

So now that he had government power, what did he do with it?

Big Government Is the Answer

Joseph's famine program began with a tax increase. The government would take twenty percent (that's one fifth if you do the math) of all the crops for the seven good years. Twenty percent sounds pretty good to me. I would gladly pay a total tax bill of only twenty percent. But to the ancient Egyptians this must have been extraordinary. Like all large government expansions throughout history, it was justified by a crisis.

The crisis was actually a real one in this case—the seven years of famine. And, indeed, the program worked. The people did not starve and there was enough seed to replant when the famine was over.

Now if you are a big government person, this may be music to your ears. *Here is biblical proof that the government should provide whatever the people need. Central planning is wonderful! And Joseph is the model of a godly leader using the power of government for a righteous end.* Case closed.

Or not. Let us continue with the narrative. When the Egyptians ran out of food, they went to the government warehouses and asked for grain. I imagine the conversation could have been something like this:

> Peasant: *I'm hungry. Give me some grain.*
>
> Official: *Okay, but you have to pay for it.*
>
> Peasant: *What do you mean "pay for it?" Where do you think that grain came from? That's the grain I've been bringing here for the last seven years.*
>
> Official: *It is Pharaoh's grain.*
>
> Peasant: *I beg to differ.*
>
> Official: *Take it or leave it. There is no other.*
>
> Peasant: *I'm going to organize a pressure group and do something about this.*
>
> Official: *Do you see Bruno over there? How would you like him to drag you behind the Sphinx and teach you a little respect?*

JOSEPH

Peasant: Hmmm. How much to fill this basket?

When the Egyptians ran out of money, Joseph took ownership of their livestock in payment for grain. When their livestock credit was depleted...

> "We will not hide from my lord that our money is all spent. The herds of livestock are my lord's. There is nothing left in the sight of my lord but our bodies and our land. Why should we die before your eyes, both we and our land? Buy us and our land for food, and we with our land will be servants to Pharaoh. And give us seed that we may live and not die, and that the land may not be desolate." So Joseph bought all the land of Egypt for Pharaoh, for all the Egyptians sold their fields, because the famine was severe on them. The land became Pharaoh's. As for the people, he made servants of them from one end of Egypt to the other.
> Genesis 47:18-21

To sum up, Joseph used the famine crisis to greatly expand the extent and control of government. Before the famine program, the common people owned livestock and land. But during the program they sold it all to the government. They were given no choice. It was that or die.

Political Smarts

What is most amazing in this story is the people's reaction. You may think that they would be angry and bitter over what their government did to them. That was not the case.

> Then Joseph said to the people, "Behold, I have this day bought you and your land for Pharaoh. Now here is seed for you, and you shall sow the land. And at the harvests you shall give a fifth to Pharaoh, and four fifths shall be your own, as seed for the field and as food for yourselves and your households, and as food for your little ones." And they said, "You have saved our lives; may it please my lord, we will be servants to Pharaoh." So Joseph made it a statute concerning the land of Egypt, and it stands to this day, that Pharaoh should have the fifth.
> Genesis 47:23-26

Notice Joseph's political skills. While making the twenty percent tax permanent, he emphasizes "four fifths shall be your own." The spin is not on what the government takes but on what it gives. The Egyptians get to keep some of what they earn. And to top it all off, Joseph throws in "as food for your little ones." Big government politicians still use this old line today. *It is for the children.*

So what is the people's response? They love Joseph! "You have saved our lives." And they joyfully accept that they have been enslaved to Pharaoh.

Joseph was a very shrewd politician.

I wonder why Joseph didn't come up with a free market solution? This would have not only retained the economic freedoms of the people but also would have eliminated the need for an expensive government infrastructure, which is the inevitable nature of public programs. In the end the people could have been both richer and freer.

I suppose that Joseph's intention all along might have been to suppress the Egyptian nation. Or maybe God told him to do it. Or…

Now you are just speculating!

You got me there. The Bible does not explain why Joseph took this course. It merely states what he did and the outcome it produced. It is descriptive not prescriptive, as they say.

While the purpose of Joseph's actions regarding the Egyptians may be unclear, the purpose is very clear when it comes to the Israelites. His brothers bowed before Joseph, of course, in fulfillment of the dream. But more importantly, he preserved the Jewish nation. In fact, he did more than merely preserve them. While the native Egyptians were being enslaved, the alien Israelites were prospering.

> Thus Israel settled in the land of Egypt, in the land of Goshen. And they gained possessions in it, and were fruitful and multiplied greatly.
>
> Genesis 47:27

Kingdom of the World—Location Egypt

One last thing about the kingdom of the world in Egypt. Pharaoh was considered to be a god by the Egyptians. He was the head of their religion, as well as the head of their government. These two institutions were not separated in Egypt. They were joined together in this man.

So?

So Joseph, who knew the true God, was willing to serve under a false one, who was the head of an idolatrous religious system.

And your point is?

I am just observing. The political situation was far from ideal. Yet

JOSEPH

Joseph participated in it from both the bottom and top levels of the power structure.

* * *

Now back to the questions I asked at the beginning of this section. Did Joseph exercise dominion in the various circumstances in which he found himself? Yes, from the bottom to the top of the authority structure in Egypt. And in these situations, is government portrayed as neutral ground? Definitely. Evil was committed against Joseph but he accomplished good. Do you see the spiritual influences of the kingdom of God and the opposing kingdom of Satan, as well as the sovereignty of God ruling over all in his everlasting kingdom? Yes, in the moral actions of the individuals and in God's guiding hand accomplishing his purposes.

I'm not going to keep repeating these questions and answering them for every chapter. This is your work to do from now on.

14 Boaz

Book of Ruth
Circa 12th Century BC

The second person up for political examination is Boaz.
Wait a minute!
What's the problem?
You skipped over Moses.
Yeah, I did.
How can you skip Moses? He is the great law giver. Who could be more important to an understanding of politics?
Don't worry. I'll get to him later.

Rotten Times

Boaz lived during the time after Joshua and before Israel had a king. This is known as the period of the judges. It was a very turbulent time politically. The twelve tribes had formed a loose national coalition, sometimes cooperating together for defense. Sometimes not. Since the judges were only appointed on an ad hoc basis, there was no permanent human ruling authority in the nation.

Here is a telling exchange between the people and one of the judges—Gideon—halfway through the book. Gideon had his faults, but he correctly understood the political order.

> Then the men of Israel said to Gideon, "Rule over us, you and your son and your grandson also, for you have saved us from the hand of Midian." Gideon said to them, "I will

> not rule over you, and my son will not rule over you; the LORD will rule over you."
>
> Judges 8:22-23

"The Lord will rule over you." Israel's civil king was God himself. Every Israelite was to self-govern under God and obey the national rules without governmental overhead.

The rules were, of course, Moses' law, the Old Covenant, their contract with God. You would think that this was the perfect setup. But the dreary history recounted in the book of Judges describes a cycle of disobedience to the rules, then oppression by foreigners, then repentance and then deliverance by a judge. Repeat.

What is striking in Israel's special and unique relationship to God was that it was such a disaster politically, as summarized in this refrain of the book of Judges.

> In those days there was no king in Israel. Everyone did what was right in his own eyes.
>
> Judges 21:25

"Everyone did what was right in his own eyes" is a description of a breakdown of government, of society, of civil order.

I find Judges to be the most discouraging and depressing book in the Bible. Even the great judges, like Sampson, are notable for their moral failings. The place was a mess!

I will attempt no explanation for this exercise of government without human rulers. My interest is in the political environment. The period of the judges provides an example of breakdown of the civil order.

So the question arises, "How should you fulfill your dominion and kingdom responsibilities in such chaotic times?" Let us observe Boaz.

A Law-Abiding Man in Lawless Times

Boaz is not found in the book of Judges. He is found in the little book of Ruth that follows Judges. I realize that some of you may be offended at my treatment of this book. After all, Ruth is a beautiful story of redemption and romance. I do not deny it. I myself find Ruth to be one of the most uplifting and encouraging books in the Bible.

But our subject is the decidedly dreary topic of politics.

Here is the beginning of the book. It is written so concisely that I am unable to compact it further.

> In the days when the judges ruled there was a famine in the land, and a man of Bethlehem in Judah went to sojourn in the country of Moab, he and his wife and his two sons. The name of the man was Elimelech and the name of his wife Naomi, and the names of his two sons were Mahlon and Chilion. They were Ephrathites from Bethlehem in Judah. They went into the country of Moab and remained there. But Elimelech, the husband of Naomi, died, and she was left with her two sons. These took Moabite wives; the name of the one was Orpah and the name of the other Ruth. They lived there about ten years, and both Mahlon and Chilion died, so that the woman was left without her two sons and her husband.
>
> Ruth 1:1-5

Life was terrible in Israel. There was famine, which was one of the curses in Moses' law for disobedience, but also it was just a rotten time politically, as I have said. So Elimelech moved his family to Moab. They were immigrants or refugees. It is always difficult to move to another country where you become the alien and must start over. This is a desperate measure usually only taken when the political climate in your own country deteriorates enough to justify the relocation.

If this was not bad enough, Naomi lost all of the breadwinners in her family—her husband and her two sons. She needed support and was unlikely to find it in Moab. And since the economy had improved in Israel, she decided to return. Ruth was determined to go with her and did so. This was certainly not a move that was calculated politically or economically. Ruth would now become an unsupported alien. But she was willing to take the risk for a better reason.

> Your people shall be my people, and your God my God.
>
> Ruth 1:16

Once in Israel the two women faced an immediate challenge. Starvation. These were rough days where hardship was not measured by the size of your television or the model of your smart phone but merely by survival. And just to take any remaining warm glow off of the situation, Ruth was a young woman who could have been easily taken advantage of.

What to do? Well, eating was at the top of the list. So Naomi sent Ruth out to glean in the fields, despite the physical danger to her. Gleaning was the law of the land because Moses' law was the law of the land. The law required landowners to leave the grain their harvesters missed in order that the poor, the alien, the widow and the fatherless could pick it up. Ruth met at least three of these qualifications.

It so "happened," which is the biblical nod to the sovereignty of God, that Ruth found herself in the field belonging to Boaz. Who was Boaz? As it so happened, as they say, he was a relative of Naomi's on her dead husband's side. When Boaz learns who Ruth is, he says this to her.

> Now, listen, my daughter, do not go to glean in another field or leave this one, but keep close to my young women. Let your eyes be on the field that they are reaping, and go after them. Have I not charged the young men not to touch you? And when you are thirsty, go to the vessels and drink what the young men have drawn.
>
> Ruth 2:8-9

Boaz addressed Ruth as "my daughter." He protects her and provides for her and Naomi's needs. This shows him to be a good fellow. More significantly for our purposes, it shows him to be a man who obeys the Mosaic law. He obeyed the letter and intent of the law.

I wonder who would have enforced the law if Boaz had not obeyed it. I suppose no one would have. This is speculation on my part, but I am probably right. Regardless of what others did, Boaz was a godly man, which means he feared God. And the fear of God results in obedience to God, which results in civil order.

The Legal Beagle

When Ruth returns with her gleanings to her mother-in-law, Naomi presses her for details. *Yeah…uh huh…Boaz, you say!* It so happened that Boaz was one of her kinsman-redeemers. What was a kinsman-redeemer? He was a member of one's extended family who could help out in a pinch.

Naomi knew the responsibilities of a kinsman-redeemer because she knew the law. So she instructs Ruth to do something that seems a bit forward to us but was within acceptable cultural practice at the time.

> See, he is winnowing barley tonight at the threshing floor. Wash therefore and anoint yourself, and put on your cloak and go down to the threshing floor, but do not make yourself known to the man until he has finished eating and drinking. But when he lies down, observe the place where he lies. Then go and uncover his feet and lie down, and he will tell you what to do.
>
> Ruth 3:2-4

Boaz, even after a hard day's work and a night of partying, realizes the significance of this action. It is a request for marriage, an appeal to redeem Elimelech's property and a commitment to continue Elimelech's family line. Again, all of this is in accordance with Moses' law.

Boaz was excited about the prospect of marriage. However, there was a problem, which he explains to Ruth. There was a kinsman-redeemer in line in front of him—one who had the first right of refusal. You would think that Boaz would overlook such legal minutia, especially when he was eager to do something so good and honorable. But no. He insisted on following the law.

Does it seem odd to you that Boaz was able to sort through all of these legal and lineage complexities immediately upon being woken up in the middle of the night by a young and attractive woman? Don't answer that. It is only my speculation. But it is safe to assume that the man had already given the scenario some consideration.

Whatever the case, Boaz initiates formal legal proceedings at the city gate the next day. He collars the unnamed kinsman-redeemer and ten elders. He suggests that the unnamed kinsman-redeemer buy Elimelech's land. The gentleman agrees to do so.

At this point the plot appears to unravel. But then Boaz points out the fine print.

> The day you buy the field from the hand of Naomi, you also acquire Ruth the Moabite, the widow of the dead, in order to perpetuate the name of the dead in his inheritance.
>
> Ruth 4:5

The unnamed kinsman-redeemer was unwilling to accept these contractual riders. The deal was off. Boaz was free to acquire the property…and a fine wife. Which he did.

* * *

Boaz and Ruth have a son. His name was Obed. Obed was the father of Jesse. Jesse was the father of David. And the generations that descended from David, as you know, included Jesus. This is by far the most significant part of the story.

But significance is not what we are focused on. We are focused on politics. And what do we learn about politics from this story? It is that even in the worst of times—even in difficult and unruly times—God blesses those who bless others by upholding social order in the kingdom of the world.

15 Obadiah

I Kings 18:1-16
9th Century BC

There are a bucketful of Obadiahs in the Bible. Obadiah was a common name. (Like Bob.) It means a "servant or worshipper of the Lord," which is an admirable quality. The most well-known Obadiah was the prophet who wrote the book known as…Obadiah, of course. But he is the wrong Obadiah for this chapter. I will focus on a minor character who makes only a cameo appearance in the book of First Kings.

Our Obadiah lived up to his name. The Scripture attests to his character.

> Now Obadiah feared the LORD greatly.
> I Kings 18:3

"Fearing the Lord" is one of the highest compliments in the Bible. It does not mean that you are terrified of God, but that you believe that he exists and will judge everything and, therefore, you obey his commands. "The fear of the Lord," as Solomon said, "is the beginning of wisdom."

Bad Boss

But there was something about Obadiah that may cause you to question his godliness and wisdom. His employer.

Obadiah worked for the wicked Ahab, king of the northern nation of Israel. Unlike Judah to the south, Israel had an unbroken succession of loser kings. But even in this gallery of rogues Ahab rose to the top of his class…or, more accurately, sunk to the bottom.

> And Ahab the son of Omri did evil in the sight of the LORD, more than all who were before him. And as if it had been a light thing for him to walk in the sins of Jeroboam the son of Nebat, he took for his wife Jezebel the daughter of Ethbaal king of the Sidonians, and went and served Baal and worshiped him. ...Ahab did more to provoke the LORD, the God of Israel, to anger than all the kings of Israel who were before him.
>
> I Kings 16:30-33

Ahab was one bad dude. And to top it off he married Jezebel, who undoubtedly became the worst queen EVER. In order to relax after her own evildoing, she would goad her husband into boosting his own score.

There is a lesson buried in here somewhere about marrying wisely. But that is not our concern. Our interest is in the government they headed. This is not difficult to characterize. Israel under their rule was spiritually dark. The land was neutral but the political activity occurring on top of it surely delighted the devil. Mr. and Mrs. Ahab's allegiance to kingdom of Satan was evident in their actions.

So what was Obadiah doing in the civil service?

Well...he was doing a good job. How do I know? Because Ahab had placed Obadiah in charge of the palace, a prominent position that would only be given to one who was trusted. And in addition to the chamberlain gig, Ahab relied upon Obadiah for other important duties...like the one coming up.

Save the Horses...and the Prophets

Here is the background. There was famine in the land, as prophesied by Elijah. Famine, as has been noted, was a curse that resulted from the Jews breaking Moses' law, their covenant with God. The northern nation of Israel was full of covenant breakers from beginning to end. But violation of the law did not invalidate the law. And so there was famine.

> And Ahab said to Obadiah, "Go through the land to all the springs of water and to all the valleys. Perhaps we may find grass and save the horses and mules alive, and not lose some of the animals." So they divided the land between them to pass through it. Ahab went in one direction by himself, and Obadiah went in another direction by himself.
>
> I Kings 18:5-6

Well, it just so happened that Obadiah wandered into Elijah. Obadiah bowed to the prophet, which seemed like a good thing to do. Elijah then commanded him to fetch his "lord" Ahab. This was awkward. Was Elijah implying something here? In any case, it unsettled Obadiah.

> "How have I sinned, that you would give your servant into the hand of Ahab, to kill me?"
>
> I Kings 18:9

Obadiah was pleading for his life. Ahab had been searching for the prophet for a long time and Elijah had always eluded him. Obadiah expected that Elijah would disappear once more and that Ahab would take his frustration out on the messenger. Knowing the king as he did, this was probably a good guess.

Now you may think that Obadiah was a sniveling coward. After all isn't it a glorious thing to die for the faith? And don't you suspect that Obadiah was a wishy-washy, lukewarm compromiser by serving in such a wicked government? Here was his opportunity to set all things right, to say what he should have said long ago. He could have confronted Ahab along these lines.

> God's prophet Elijah summons you—you wicked excuse for a king. Make haste! Go to him. He will probably be gone by the time you arrive but so what. Your false gods and their prophets cannot help you now. In fact, they have never helped you. Duh! Neither can that vile woman you call your wife. And now I remove this little pin from my robe that you gave me for ten years of faithful service. I throw it on the ground! I spit on it! I stamp on it! I rue every moment I served in your evil government! Here is my neck. I stretch it out for you. Lop off my head and so remove my shame!

But no. Obadiah did not have such a death wish. He did not seek to antagonize the state. He did not long for the glory of an entry in *Foxe's Book of Martyrs*. He wanted to live, which is a healthy human desire.

This was the consistent practice of godly people throughout the Bible. Not one of them antagonized the government in order to provoke their own death. Some were killed, as you know. But there is a difference between dying for the faith when there is no way of honorable escape and using the state as the instrument of your suicide.

Besides, I will remind you of the consistent biblical instruction regarding your political objective. It is not drama. It is not martyrdom.

> First of all, then, I urge that supplications, prayers, intercessions, and thanksgivings be made for all people, for kings and all who are in high positions, that we may **lead a peaceful and quiet life**, godly and dignified in every way.
>
> I Timothy 2:1-2

The Sneaky Palace Keeper

Now back to our man in I Kings. There was more to the seemingly milquetoast Obadiah than first meets the eye. He had a bit of the heroic in him after all. You may disapprove of his government position, but it did have some advantages. And he made the most of them.

> Has it not been told my lord [Elijah] what I did when Jezebel killed the prophets of the LORD, how I hid a hundred men of the LORD's prophets by fifties in a cave and fed them with bread and water?
>
> I Kings 18:13

Saving the prophets was pretty gutsy when that terror of a queen was out trying to kill them. It is not likely that she knew what Obadiah was up to because she was the type that would have done something about it. Did the king endorse her purge? Perhaps slaughtering God's prophets was going too far for him. We do not know. But Obadiah expected that Elijah had heard the news. "Has it not been told my lord."

And there is another thing. Obadiah "fed them with bread and water." This was even more dangerous and difficult than hiding the prophets. Why? Because there was a desperate famine in the land. In these circumstances food and water is usually controlled and rationed. Where would Obadiah obtain them? Well, he was in charge of the king's household, which was the first place groceries were delivered.

I'm Not Going to Do That

This brings us to the issue I have long avoided. Is it ever right to disobey government rulers and rules?

It's about time.

Let me begin by making another distinction. The biblical command to obey rulers and rules is not an absolute command. It is a general command. What is the difference? There are no exceptions to an absolute command. If a ruler says to kill the prophets, you are required to kill them. Obey your rulers, no matter what. Always. But a general command means that there are exceptions and that disobedience is the right thing to do in certain limited circumstances.

Let's zoom out from a focus on politics once again in order to apply this concept to the other dominion institutions of family and employment.

Do you interpret the command for wives to submit to their husbands as an absolute command? Should a wife never disobey her husband…even when he tells her to do something immoral? I hope not! Or should children always obey parents? What if parents require Junior to kneecap Billy from across the street because the little brat knocked a baseball through the living room window? Or should employees unquestioningly follow the boss's orders? *I want you to slash all the tires in the MegaMart parking lot so that people will start shopping here instead.*

The biblical requirement to obey human rulers is a general command. This includes government rulers. Why? Because every individual in a ruling position has received the authority to rule from God. Authority from God comes with accountability to God for ruling with justice.

When a ruler refuses to rule with justice, the ruled are no longer required to submit. The ruler has no authority from God to impose injustice. In other words, a ruler cannot legitimately issue a rule that violates God's standards.

If he does, the ruled have the responsibility to disobey. Why? Because every person is accountable to God to live righteously, not just the rulers. Jesus will judge the ruled for their political response to injustice, as he will judge the rulers for their actions.

This should not be a surprise. You sense instinctively that this is true. It is part of the moral nature you inherited when the human race was created in the image of God. It is not because you are a Christian that this seems right. It is because you are a human.

Consider as an example the Nuremburg Trials after World War II. Some Nazi leaders were tried for certain war crimes and crimes against humanity. The *I-was-ordered-to-do-it* defense was not accepted. That was right. Their obligation to the Führer did not override their obligation to God.

But having said this, it is also true that while you may be justified in disobeying the government in one area does not mean that you may disobey the government in other areas. Nope. No free pass. Obadiah opposed the killing of the prophets, but he did not have a license to line his pockets from the royal treasury, for example.

The Midwife Subversion

I must admit that the passage about Obadiah provides no judgement about whether his actions were right or wrong. There is only a record of what he said and did, without comment. So I am interpreting the passage when I assume that he did the right thing by saving the prophets.

But I think that I am on solid ground. Consider another biblical scenario where a ruler was disobeyed. The setting was the birth of Moses.

Now are you going to talk about Moses?

Quit interrupting. Pharaoh had commanded the Hebrew midwives to kill all of the baby boys. This they refused to do so. They even lied about it. *Pharaoh, you know how vigorous those women are. They pop those boys out like little cannon balls before we can get there!*

Here is God's response.

> So God dealt well with the midwives. And the people multiplied and grew very strong. And because the midwives feared God, he gave them families.
> Exodus 1:20-21

The actions of the midwives pleased God. How do we know? Because he blessed them. And did you catch the phrase "the midwives feared God?" This was high praise, but not as high as Obadiah received. He feared the Lord "greatly."

It is also evident that Pharaoh's decree to kill the boys was unjust. This was murder plain and simple. It was done to achieve a political objective—to insure that the Hebrews did not grow too powerful. But Pharaoh was accountable to God to rule justly. When he did not, the midwives responded appropriately.

The Ruler's Rules

There is also a legal aspect of Obadiah's circumstances that differs from the midwives' case. Pharaoh—being a god, supposedly, or at least the intermediary to the gods—made the law of the land. There was no disconnect between this ruler and his rules.

But what were the rules in Israel? Were they Ahab's decrees? No, they were not. They were Moses' laws. The fact that Ahab disobeyed these rules did not alter their legal standing. Israel was in a covenant relationship with God and no king had the right to unilaterally alter the covenant. And in case Ahab forgot this detail, God sent his prophets to remind him of it.

In Israel the ruler was subject to the rules. No one was above the law of the land. Obadiah was actually upholding the law by preventing the unlawful murdering of God's prophets.

* * *

Anyway, I think it is obvious that Obadiah did the right thing by saving the prophets. So I will belabor his story no longer.

Next I will examine the politics of another fellow. He is, perhaps, the most unlikely political operative of all time. He did not want the assignment from God. He refused to go at first. And although he eventually grudgingly complied, he wasn't happy with the outcome…even though his mission was a complete success. He is not a sterling example of faithfulness in his kingdom of the world responsibilities. But then again, you and I probably aren't either.

.

16 Jonah

Book of Jonah
8th Century BC

Am I persuading you of the importance of politics and of your responsibilities in the public realm? Or do you think this is a useless task, wasted effort, spitting into the wind, putting lipstick on a pig?

And won't any attempt at civil reformation distract people from their "soul" needs? After all, times of peace and prosperity just foster spiritually apathy, don't they? Best to let wickedness run its course so that they get a little taste of hell. That medicine will actually do them some good.

Besides, if the idolaters are busy swindling and killing each other, they will have less time to cause trouble for God's people. Right?

Hello, Jonah.

* * *

The book of Jonah is more than a fish story. It is the tale of a man who did not want to engage in politics for the public good. It is the account of the improbable improvement of a wicked government. And, of course, it is an illustration of God sovereignly working for good in the kingdom of the world.

It begins on an evil note.

> Now the word of the LORD came to Jonah the son of Amittai, saying, "Arise, go to Nineveh, that great city, and call out against it, for their evil has come up before me."
> Jonah 1:1-2

It was not unusual for God to send his prophets to warn his chosen people of the political disaster awaiting them if they refused to repent of their evil ways and live righteously. What was unusual was that he sent Jonah on special assignment to the pagan nation of Assyria with this message.

Assyrians Are Humans Too

In the passage above, God gives the reason for his focus on Nineveh, the capital of Assyria. "Their evil has come up before me." You may be wondering why this merited attention. After all, weren't all of the pagan nations full of evil? Yes, they were. Just read through the rest of the prophets to confirm that. Why was God even concerned about Assyria? Israel was his chosen nation.

To begin with, the God of the Bible is not a local deity. He is king of the everlasting kingdom, which encompasses all nations. And although the Old Covenant, Moses' law, did not apply to Assyria, the Dominion Mandate did. The Assyrians (like everyone else) were required to rule righteously. In this they were failing. So God called them on it.

There seems to be a threshold of evil that, if exceeded, draws the wrath of God in the form of national judgement.[12] The Ninevites had passed that boundary.

> Yet forty days, and Nineveh shall be overthrown!
> Jonah 3:4

That was Jonah's prophecy against Assyria. It was a warning about political destruction. Very concise. Very precise. Forty days. The clock was ticking. Strong stuff.

Jonah's Hang-Up

Why did Jonah resist his assignment from God? Well, no one enjoys being the bearer of bad news. And there is that saying about shooting the messenger. The Assyrians were not a gentle people. But I do not think concern for his personal safety is what most alarmed the prophet.

The context of the book points toward something else. Jonah feared that the Assyrians would repent of their wickedness and that God would spare them national destruction. The prophet knew that God poured

---

[12] This principle is also illustrated in Genesis 18:20-21 regarding the judgement of Sodom and Gomorrah.

bucketfuls of his mercy on Israel, but he did not want the Assyrians to get a drop of it.

If God was merciful to Assyria, there were serious political consequences for Israel. Hosea had prophesied that Assyria would rule over Israel.[13] Jonah would have been aware of this. So here is his likely political calculus. *God told me to warn the Assyrians of impending judgement. If I do that, they may repent of their wickedness. If they repent, God will show them mercy and not destroy their nation. If they are not destroyed, they will be able to defeat and exile Israel according to the prophecies. Therefore, in order to protect Israel, I will not deliver God's warning to them.* This was shrewd political logic.

But God was persistent and insistent that Jonah deliver the message. And, as the story goes, Jonah eventually complied.

And then his worst fears were realized.

> And the people of Nineveh believed God. They called for a fast and put on sackcloth, from the greatest of them to the least of them. The word reached the king of Nineveh, and he arose from his throne, removed his robe, covered himself with sackcloth, and sat in ashes. And he issued a proclamation and published through Nineveh, "By the decree of the king and his nobles: Let neither man nor beast, herd nor flock, taste anything. Let them not feed or drink water, but let man and beast be covered with sackcloth, and let them call out mightily to God. Let everyone turn from his evil way and from the violence that is in his hands."
>
> Jonah 3:5-8

Note the last sentence. "Let everyone turn from his evil way and from the violence that is in his hands." This refers to civil order, to law, to government. In other words, *It's time to clean up our act, folks.*

The king of Nineveh ends with this very interesting sentence.

> Who knows? God may turn and relent and turn from his fierce anger, so that we may not perish.
>
> Jonah 3:9

This is how Jonah understood his prophecy. It was not a declaration about what was inevitable but a warning of the consequences of not repenting. And the next verse proves that they were right.[14]

---

[13] See Hosea 9:3 and 11:5.

[14] There are many examples of the conditional nature of some prophecies.

> When God saw what they did, how they turned from their evil way, God relented[15] of the disaster that he had said he would do to them, and he did not do it.
>
> Jonah 3:10

Now look at this from another angle. Being a prophet was kind of a lousy job. Nothing but grief. Customer appreciation was usually nonexistent. But here, for once, was the response every prophet dreamed about. The people believed God and repented! Imagine if Jonah had gotten this reaction in Israel.

But we learn in the last chapter that he was not happy one bit.

> But it displeased Jonah exceedingly, and he was angry. And he prayed to the LORD and said, "O LORD, is not this what I said when I was yet in my country? That is why I made haste to flee to Tarshish; for I knew that you are a gracious God and merciful, slow to anger and abounding in steadfast love, and relenting from disaster. Therefore now, O LORD, please take my life from me, for it is better for me to die than to live."
>
> Jonah 4:1-3

Exodus 32:14 and Jeremiah 36:3 are two of them.

[15] Some take this statement that "God relented" (and others like it) as support for the idea that man's choices are unknown to God, who must continually alter his plans in response. They would interpret the passage this way: *God decided to punish the Ninevites for their wickedness. So he sent Jonah down there so that they would know what was going to hit them. The Ninevites upon hearing the message repented—a response that surprised God and caused him to cancel his planned judgement upon them.* The idea behind this theology is that man cannot make real choices if God is truly sovereign over all. In kingdom terminology, this is saying that the kingdom of the world cannot exist within the everlasting kingdom. That is a false premise. And then to correct this presumed error, they make a worse one—stripping God of his sovereignty and imaging that he must respond to the whims of man, as if God was a puppeteer controlled by the movements of his puppets. Better to understand Jonah's prophecy simply as a warning that the Ninevites had better fulfill their dominion responsibilities righteously or face God's judgement. It was not an unveiling of God's plan...which turned out to be wrong. The concept of God's sovereignty is not difficult to understand. It is hard to accept. Why? Because it is humbling to man, who since Genesis 3 has yearned to rule over God not under him. But God gives grace to the humble, as even a pagan king discovered.

Jonah may have had some good qualities...but they are not revealed to us. His response was really pathetic.

He was given a mission directly from God—to engage this people, this corrupt culture, to prod them to rule themselves justly. But no. Jonah wanted no part of it. He wanted their destruction. So God rebuked him.

> And should not I pity Nineveh, that great city, in which there are more than 120,000 persons who do not know their right hand from their left, and also much cattle?"
> Jonah 4:11

Ouch!

The Political Lesson

As Jonah feared, Assyria became the rod of God's punishment for Israel. But then, after they relapsed into wickedness, they too fell by the sword.[16] All nations rise and fall according to God's plan within his everlasting kingdom.

Does this mean that Jonah's assignment was useless? Because Assyria's political reformation was not permanent, was it was not worth doing?

Let's play that out. What political order is permanent? In fact, what effort of any kind in this life is "one and done?" Take the most mundane of examples. Why make your bed this morning when you are going to mess it up again tonight? Why take a shower today when you will need another tomorrow? If you put effort into transitory personal order, shouldn't you be willing to put some into the evolving public order?

The repentance of the Ninevites was not for nothing. It made a difference to those who were suffering under the violence of injustice at that time. After all, these were people created in the image of God. They counted for something.

So do your neighbors.

---

[16] See the book of Nahum. This is the second Old Testament prophetical book directed at the Assyrians. Unfortunately, they did not heed God's warning and repent of their wickedness this time. So they suffered the consequences.

17 Daniel

The Book of Daniel
6th Century BC

Daniel's story is similar to Joseph's in many ways. He too could be the hero in a Horatio Alger tale, which always begin with some misfortune.

Daniel's misfortune was political disaster. Nebuchadnezzar, king of Babylon, had invaded and defeated Judah. Nebuchadnezzar famously looted some vessels from the temple, which show up again later in the book, but he also took something else. Captives.

I suspect that these served as hostages in order to ensure Judah's subservience to their new overlord. There was also another purpose. They were candidates for the civil service. And they were good ones.

> Then the king commanded Ashpenaz, his chief eunuch, to bring some of the people of Israel, both of the royal family and of the nobility, youths without blemish, of good appearance and skillful in all wisdom, endowed with knowledge, understanding learning, and competent to stand in the king's palace, and to teach them the literature and language of the Chaldeans.
>
> Daniel 1:3-4

These were the type of kids that are profiled every year as the "best and brightest" among high school graduates—kids that are valedictorians, letter in five sports, and spend the summer building windmills in the Sahara. These Jewish boys were from privilege, from the elite of Israeli society.

Upon arriving in Babylon they were enrolled in preparatory school for three years. Then they were examined by the king himself, which must have been a terrifying experience. I imagine that those who failed muster would find themselves employed in cleaning the royal stables, despite their stellar résumés. But that was not the fate of Daniel and his three friends.

> God gave them learning and skill in all literature and wisdom, and Daniel had understanding in all visions and dreams. …And the king spoke with them, and among all of them none was found like Daniel, Hananiah, Mishael, and Azariah. Therefore they stood before the king. And in every matter of wisdom and understanding about which the king inquired of them, he found them ten times better than all the magicians and enchanters that were in all his kingdom.
>
> Daniel 1:17-20

Now let us step back and view this from a political perspective. Look at the intolerable conditions. Those poor children! Ripped from their mothers' arms, trotted across the desert to some strange pagan land, and subjected to tremendous academic pressure.

And did you notice the course load? Daniel and his friends were "ten times better than all the magicians and enchanters that were in all his kingdom." Magicians? Enchanters? Hmmm. Just like in the Egypt of Joseph's day, pagan religion was all mixed into government.

Have I enraged your sense of justice? How would you respond in such circumstances? Would you resist actively or at least passively? Would you try to escape? How about assassinate the king?

It is clear what Daniel did. He thrived within the system. He mastered the course load. He fully applied himself despite the less than ideal circumstances.

Do you think that he did what was right? Well, no matter. God approved, since he gave Daniel "learning and skill in all literature and wisdom."

Dieting in Babylon

Hey, you skipped over something. If Daniel was so into Babylonian culture, why did he make such a fuss about the food?

Good catch. Let's look at that.

> But Daniel resolved that he would not defile himself with the king's food, or with the wine that he drank.
>
> Daniel 1:8

DANIEL

The civil service preparatory school was designed to shape the whole person. Mind and body. That is, it required an intake of food and drink from the royal cafeteria, as well as intellectual knowledge from the professors.

The problem for Daniel may have been a violation the dietary laws of the Old Covenant or perhaps the pagan practice of offering the first portion of food and drink to idols. In any case, Daniel assumed that he would be defiled.

This raises the question of jurisdiction. Which set of rules was Daniel obligated to obey? Israel's or Babylon's? Or both? And if there was a conflict, which took precedent?

These are difficult questions. In addition to diet, consider the myriad of complexities that Daniel faced over Sabbath or temple sacrifices or even tassels on his clothing. How were these requirements of Moses' law to be observed…or not?

The Jews—having been scattered throughout the earth for much of their history—have given a great deal of thought to these questions, which are their riddles to solve, not mine. I only mention them to illustrate the perplexities of being subject to more than one set of rules.

In fact, you may very well find yourself in a situation where you must obey rules of another government. It's easy. Live in a country in which you are not a citizen. Or just travel there. The authorities will not give a hoot if your own laws require you to drive on the right side of the road. In their country you will drive on the left. Upon violation, you may argue the absolute absurdity of this to the magistrate (and rightly so, I say) until you are blue in the face. It will make no difference. You are subject to the law of the land.

At the same time, you are still subject to the rules of your own country. I think not of those nagging traffic laws but of more serious ones. For example, you cannot sell uranium to the North Koreans even if you are vacationing in Pyongyang and the locals are all for it.

You may think that I have chased the rabbits here. After all, isn't this chapter about Daniel in Babylon? Why have I created a fictional idiot and put him in North Korea?

I concede the point.

My argument is only that obeying rulers and rules in the kingdom of the world is a challenge. It will not be so in the next world under a single great King and his kingdom. But you are stuck here for now and must figure out how to live righteously in all of the crosscurrents.

Salad Bar Please

Unfortunately, Daniel did not write one of those books that neatly sorted this all out. *Babylonian Lessons: Ten Principles that Easily and Quickly Clarify Every Impossibly Complex Conundrum Surrounding Rulers and Rules.* Nope. But he did do something better.

Daniel demonstrated a wise approach to rulers about a rule that violated his conscience. He sought an exemption to the rule.

> Therefore he asked the chief of the eunuchs to allow him not to defile himself.
>
> Daniel 1:8

Have you heard the saying, "It is better to ask for forgiveness than to ask for permission?" I love that saying and have quoted it often. It seems especially fitting when you are bogged down in a swamp of unnecessary rules. However, I must admit, this path of least resistance is not the one that Daniel chose. He did not secretively slide the pork chops under the pillows. Instead, he appealed to his immediate supervisor.

In response, the chief of the eunuchs pointed out a technical problem with the plan.

> I fear my lord the king, who assigned your food and your drink; for why should he see that you were in worse condition than the youths who are of your own age? So you would endanger my head with the king.
>
> Daniel 1:10

But Daniel had anticipated this. He proposed a solution that would benefit his boss instead of endanger him.

> Test your servants for ten days; let us be given vegetables to eat and water to drink. Then let our appearance and the appearance of the youths who eat the king's food be observed by you, and deal with your servants according to what you see.
>
> Daniel 1:12-13

And, according to the text, Daniel and his friends passed the trial. They looked better and were "fatter in flesh," which was apparently a good thing back then. The appeal to authority resolved the moral conflict caused by the rule.

But an exemption is not always possible.

Moving Up

Before describing Daniel's second rule conflict, I will briefly trace his governmental career path.

As you know, it began under Nebuchadnezzar, the king of Babylon. Daniel's big break occurred when the king dreamed a dream about a huge statue. The king, perhaps sensing that he would be played by his advisors, refused to tell them the dream. When they could not describe it, he ordered them all killed. Thus was his direct manner of ruling.

This created a political crisis. And a political crisis, as every good politician knows, presents danger to the ruling class but also opportunity. If one is sacked, there will be a vacancy in that nice corner office.

Daniel and his three friends were among the king's advisors, although buried deep within the bureaucracy, no doubt. When Daniel is served his death sentence, he volunteers to interpret the dream. And so he does, giving credit to the God who rules over his everlasting kingdom. As a result, Nebuchadnezzar acknowledges the greater King and promotes Daniel.

> Then the king gave Daniel high honors and many great gifts, and made him ruler over the whole province of Babylon and chief prefect over all the wise men of Babylon.
>
> Daniel 2:48

So like Joseph, Daniel rises to the top tier of government through the interpretation of a dream. A few chapters later he interprets Nebuchadnezzar's second dream. The Babylonian ruler had forgotten the theological lesson of the first dream—that God is sovereign over all—and was required to learn it again, this time with more humility.

The next we hear of Daniel is during the reign of Belshazzar, the last king of Babylon. He does not have a dream but sees the "handwriting on the wall" in an experience that originated the phrase. Daniel seems to have been retired at this point, or at least buried again in the bureaucracy, because the king is unaware of his history. In any case, Daniel is quickly dusted off and brought before the king.

Belshazzar offers Daniel a return to political power if he can interpret the frightening graffiti. He declines the gifts but interprets the writing. Daniel first delivers another lecture on the sovereignty of God and one's proper response to it. Then he said that it was all up for the Babylonians and that the Medes and Persians were taking over.

Despite the content of the message, the king was impressed. And the king's favors cannot be refused.

> Then Belshazzar gave the command, and Daniel was clothed with purple, a chain of gold was put around his neck, and a proclamation was made about him, that he should be the third ruler in the kingdom.
>
> Daniel 5:29

Normally this would be a good thing politically. But given the circumstances, I can see why Daniel preferred to forego the promotion. That very night the Medes and Persians attacked and killed Belshazzar.

Can you picture the situation? The enemy soldiers, their swords wet with the blood of the king. Daniel newly dressed in the finery of third ruler. "Hey fellas," he might have said, "I just got all this stuff tonight. No kidding." The soldiers frenzied in victory. The bloodlust shinning in their eyes. "I'm the one who said you guys would win."

In other words, it was a bit of a tricky situation. So are the ups and downs of political life.

However, the most amazing part of the story is not that Daniel lived but what happened next.

A New Administration

Darius the Mede became the ruling king.

Standard practice in setting up a new government is to "clean house," that is, to get your own people into the positions of power and influence. The incumbents usually retain some loyalty to and yearning for the old regime. They may attempt to undermine the new administration.

But Darius made a daring appointment.

> It pleased Darius to set over the kingdom 120 satraps, to be throughout the whole kingdom; and over them three high officials, of whom Daniel was one, to whom these satraps should give account, so that the king might suffer no loss.
>
> Daniel 6:1-2

You would think that if Daniel received any position, it would be along the "special advisor" lines, since he knew the ins and outs of the former Babylonian empire. He would be of use during the transition period.

But no. That was not what Darius wanted. He made Daniel a "high official." Why? "So that the king might suffer no loss." Darius wanted good government. And for that he knew that he needed officials under him that would not be corrupted. Corruption eats away at a government, like termites in the woodwork, until it is destroyed.

How did he know that he could trust Daniel in such a key role? Undoubtedly Daniel's character was well-known, as his background check quickly verified. And so the king was not disappointed.

> Then this Daniel became distinguished above all the other high officials and satraps, because an excellent spirit was in him. And the king planned to set him over the whole kingdom.
>
> Daniel 6:3

Before continuing with the narrative, let us pause to think about a few things. For one, Daniel keeps advancing. The cream rises to the top of the milk, as the yokels say. Or as the pithy Solomon said, "Do you see a man skillful in his work? He will stand before kings" (Proverbs 22:29). For a second, Daniel is doing so in several different governments. This aspect his biography surpasses Joseph's.

But opposition soon arises. Of course it did. Evil always opposes good and vice versa. There is a continuous spiritual battle.

> Then the high officials and the satraps sought to find a ground for complaint against Daniel with regard to the kingdom, but they could find no ground for complaint or any fault, because he was faithful, and no error or fault was found in him.
>
> Daniel 6:4

In case you are not following the thread here, let me recap. Daniel was in the Babylonian government. The Medes and Persians conquered them but somehow Daniel ended up in one of the top three administrative positions of the new government. Now the king is going to appoint Daniel over the entire empire.

Place yourselves in the shoes of the other high officials. A little jealousy, perhaps? *We have served the king through thick and thin. We camped out on the military campaign for months on end. We ate those lousy Meals Ready to Eat until we were sick of them. We stormed the infernal hanging gardens of Babylon. And now we will have to report to this old Jew, this retread, Mr. Squeaky Clean? We think not!*

And so they devised a plan.

> We shall not find any ground for complaint against this Daniel unless we find it in connection with the law of his God.
>
> Daniel 6:5

Notice that they could not "find any ground of complaint." That is, they scoured the law books to find some technicality that Daniel had violated. This is a testimony to good law, at least in the area of freedom of worship. Daniel's practice of Moses' law did not conflict with the law of the land.

But the officials were determined to entrap Daniel on legal grounds. So they did what politicians often do to gain an advantage in political warfare. They made a new law. A bad one.

> "O King Darius, live forever! All the high officials of the kingdom, the prefects and the satraps, the counselors and the governors are agreed that the king should establish an ordinance and enforce an injunction, that whoever makes petition to any god or man for thirty days, except to you, O king, shall be cast into the den of lions."
>
> Daniel 6:6-7

Now having a little experience in the civil service myself, I can recognize certain tactics when I see them. I recognize them because…I must admit…that I used them a time or two myself.

It goes like this. You take in a pile of paperwork to the boss. The thing he is most interested in is on top and you spend half your time talking about that. Then topic two. Then topic three. Now your time is almost up. You quickly summarize topic four. The boss is looking at his watch. You know that the eunuch in charge of the harem is waiting at the door to discuss next year's budget. You see that the boss is apprehensive about that meeting—no doubt because of all the complaining and nagging that he will receive from all of his wives and concubines. Then—at the last moment—you say, "O Boss, live forever! Just sign this last one. It's nothing more than a little strengthening of social cohesion…everyone praying only to you for a month…you know, the usual sort of thing…or being thrown into the lion's den. No big deal. Sign on the line…right there."

Did you notice that the real intent and target of the law was not mentioned? Darius probably was not paying a whole lot of attention either. And so he signed the law.

No Way Out

Now we see Daniel in an ethical dilemma a second time. Should he obey the law of the Medes and Persians or the "law of his God?" The choice was not difficult.

> When Daniel knew that the document had been signed, he went to his house where he had windows in his upper chamber open toward Jerusalem. He got down on his knees three times a day and prayed and gave thanks before his God, as he had done previously.
>
> Daniel 6:10

Daniel did not flout his disobedience to the law. He was not looking for a fight. But he continued his private practice of worship. His rivals knew he would, which again revealed the quality of Daniel's character and his public testimony. So they were able to easily catch him in the act.

Then they hurried to Darius and reminded him of the law he had signed. Interestingly, in that society the law was unalterable. It could not be repealed, even by the king. *Lex rex.* Law is king, not *Rex lex.* King is law. Daniel did not seek an exemption because there was no provision for an exemption. And Darius, whether he wanted to or not, was forced to carry out the sentence.

God saved Daniel from the lions, as you know. As for Darius, he was not amused by the political scheming to eliminate his Number Two. And so he threw the plotters and their families into the lion's den.

No Harm, No Foul

The most significant political statement in the book comes when Darius asks Daniel if he survived the night in the lion's den. Here is the reply.

> "My God sent his angel and shut the lions' mouths, and they have not harmed me, because I was found blameless before him; and also before you, O king, I have done no harm."
>
> Daniel 6:22

Even though Daniel had violated the civil law, he was "blameless" before God. Also, he had "done no harm" to the king who had issued the law. How could this be?

Let's take these two statements one at a time.

In the Obadiah chapter I made a distinction about God's command to obey rulers. It is not an absolute command. It is a general command. That is, you may disobey a human ruler or rules if they are in violation of God's requirement for justice within his everlasting kingdom. Only God's absolute standards require absolute obedience.

Once again. You should generally obey human rulers because their authority is from God. But you should always—without exception—obey

God because his overall authority takes precedent over his delegated authority when there is a conflict.

So I will add a few notes to my kingdom diagram (without the spiritual kingdom overlays).

This concept of a higher and overriding authority is also demonstrated in the book of Acts. The Jewish leaders commanded the Apostles to stop preaching the good news about Jesus. But the Apostles had been commanded *by* Jesus to spread the Gospel.

> But Peter and the apostles answered, "We must obey God rather than men."
>
> Acts 5:29

The apostles understood the relationships between the kingdoms and their responsibility to each.

So did Daniel.

He was "blameless" before God even though he broke the civil law. Obedience to God always trumps human rules that would require disobedience to him. Clear enough. But it is harder to interpret the second statement: "...and also before you, O king, I have done no harm."

Whether or not Darius realized the implications of the law or was hoodwinked into signing it makes no difference. It was an order issued by the king. He owned it.

General observation: All political power is dependent upon enforcing the rules. Breaking the rules is a threat to the ruler. If Darius did not enforce the rules, he was not ruling. If Darius failed to rule, someone else would rise up, push him out of the way and do the job. So when Daniel disobeyed the prayer order, he defied the king and threatened his position as ruler.

But Daniel insisted that he had not "harmed" Darius?

How to resolve this dilemma?

The surface answer is that because Darius executed the law, such as it was, and threw Daniel into the lion's den, he was not harmed politically. This is true enough, as confirmed by the biblical narrative.

But there is a deeper answer. Daniel's actions did not harm Darius personally.

The Second Greatest Commandment

Darius was responsible before God to rule justly. In issuing the unjust prayer order, he violated that charter. In other words, he sinned. All sin is an offense against both man and God. Therefore, sin has both temporal and eternal consequences. Consider, for example, a criminal's crime. Not only is the perpetrator threatened with prison in this life, but he is guaranteed judgement in the next. Sin is self-destructive behavior.

So Daniel did not harm Darius. Darius harmed himself.

What did Daniel do? He loved the king.

Come again?

Doing what is right is always an expression of love for God…and your neighbor. These two loves never oppose each other. They always work together.

There is a great destructive lie today that if you even disapprove of a person's behavior, then you "hate" that person. That may be the case, but it depends upon what behavior you are disapproving. If the person is harming himself and others by his actions—that is, if he is sinning—then you are not hating him but loving him by your resistance. Why? Because your action reminds him that what he is doing or has done is wrong, which is a good thing.

Call it "tough love," which is appropriate because this will probably be tough both on him and on you.

More on this later.

To return to our story, Darius responded to the news that Daniel had been caught in the prayer dragnet. He was "greatly distressed" and made "every effort to rescue him." This is not the usual reaction of a ruler who has had his authority challenged. But it is the reaction of a man who regrets the wrong he has done and wants to make amends.

Coming Full Circle

So what was the result of all of this political drama? Let us see.

> Then King Darius wrote to all the peoples, nations, and languages that dwell in all the earth: "Peace be multiplied to you. I make a decree, that in all my royal dominion people are to tremble and fear before the God of Daniel, for he is the living God, enduring forever; his kingdom shall never be destroyed, and his dominion shall be to the end."
>
> Daniel 6:25-26

Daniel's political involvement resulted in praise to God and acknowledgment of his everlasting kingdom. Not just by one pagan king but by two of them. And not just privately but publically. They told everyone under their rule.

Does that ring a bell? Think back to the beginning of this book, to the discussion of dominion. Why should you faithfully fulfill your dominion responsibilities?

The Apostle Peter knew.

> Keep your conduct among the Gentiles honorable, so that when they speak against you as evildoers, they may see your good deeds and **glorify God** on the day of visitation.
>
> I Peter 2:12

Even in this fallen world, even with the spiritual conflict raging, you are to glorify God. And even if others do not glorify God now (as Nebuchadnezzar and Darius did), they will later.

One last thing. Do you know what verse comes after the one above?

> Be subject for the Lord's sake to every human institution....
>
> I Peter 2:13

18 Esther

The Book of Esther
5th Century BC

You may be wondering about my biographical selections. Where are the political women? I have not featured any...except for a brief mention of the despicable Jezebel. She was a strong woman, which may please you, but she used her strength for evil, which should not.

Are there no noble women who instruct us about politics? Of course there are. Which brings us to Esther. She was both good and strong.

The Other Woman

But first, the book of Esther actually begins with another woman. Vashti. She was a queen. Her husband was Xerxes (also known as Ahasuerus), the son of Darius, the noteworthy ruler from our last chapter.

In the opening scene Xerxes throws a fabulous party for all of the big wigs from across his vast empire. On the seventh day of the party when Xerxes was "merry with wine," he orders his eunuchs to bring the queen so that she may "show the peoples and the princes her beauty, for she was lovely to look at."

This is not a text that should be expounded upon during family devotions with young children present. To put it bluntly, all the men were pretty well soused and the king had the bright idea to display his wife to them. *Feast your eyes on what I've got, boys!* It requires little imagination to create the drunken, leering scene that would follow.

But Vashti refused to participate in the fun. Little wonder. This would have been a degrading and shameful situation for her. In response to her no-show, the king, in whatever state of inebriation he had achieved, was enraged.

Let me bring in a wise marriage counselor at this point.

> You two have hit a rough patch. But if you are willing to work through this incident, there may be reconciliation. Xerxes, I will begin with you. You are to love your wife. What did you say? Of course, I am aware of your splitting headache and will speak more softly. But you have not loved your wife in this. Vashti, have you respected your husband and submitted to him? Although I agree with you that he crossed the line here, you must realize that you have shamed him in front of his friends and subordinates. Etc....

But the situation could not be confined to the privacy of a counselor's office.

There is an idea nowadays that the personal affairs of a politician are of no concern to the public. *His private life is none of your business and makes no difference to how he conducts his official duties.* This tactic is usually employed by the allies of a politician seeking to limit the damage of his immoral behavior. But this seldom works, which is why a politician's enemies are always eager to discuss his failings.

The point is that there are no hard lines separating public life from private life or one dominion ruler-ruled relationship from another. This is especially true for a prominent and influential ruler, who the ruled look to not only to provide justice but also as an example of acceptable behavior.

Xerxes, although apparently blind to his own boorishness, grasped this dynamic. His advisors were realists in this matter too.

> Then the king said to the wise men who knew the times (for this was the king's procedure toward all who were versed in law and judgment, the men next to him being...the seven princes of Persia and Media.... "According to the law, what is to be done to Queen Vashti, because she has not performed the command of King Ahasuerus [Xerxes] delivered by the eunuchs?" Then Memucan said in the presence of the king and the officials, "Not only against the king has Queen Vashti done wrong, but also against all the officials and all the peoples who are in all the provinces of King Ahasuerus. For the queen's behavior will be made known to all women, causing them to look at their husbands with contempt, since they will say, 'King Ahasuerus

> commanded Queen Vashti to be brought before him, and she did not come.' This very day the noble women of Persia and Media who have heard of the queen's behavior will say the same to all the king's officials, and there will be contempt and wrath in plenty.
>
> Esther 1:13-18

Note carefully the issue addressed by the advisors. It was not about what the king did but what the queen did. They were shrewd not to issue an opinion about the king's action. *If you weren't such a jerk, none of this would have happened...O Exalted One.* That would have been the end of their political careers.

They were focused solely on the fallout that would result from the queen's disobedience. They warned that widespread marriage disorder would result in a larger civil disorder. And they were right.

What!

I know that it is fashionable today to despise the ruling-ruled relationship within marriage as oppressive to women. But what is worse than abuse of rulership is the denial of it.

A leaderless marriage works no better than a leaderless workplace or a leaderless government, which is a contradiction in terms. And you should know from observation that marriage breakdown hurts everyone in the family and impacts the larger social structure of the community. Family dysfunction cannot be contained within some "private" sphere.

Stable nations rest upon the foundation of stable families. Government always has an interest in maintaining family order. This has been evident throughout history, our "enlightened" times being an exception.

> He [Xerxes] sent letters to all the royal provinces...that every man be **master** [or ruler] in his own household.
>
> Esther 1:22

Government policies exert influence—either for good or evil—upon families just as they do upon businesses. Xerxes chose to reinforce dominion order for the benefit of the empire.

As for Vashti, she was canned as queen. Was this completely fair to her? I think not. Was it absolutely clean? Nope. But politics rarely are.

Enter Esther

Vashti's exit provided a vacancy in the first family. A new queen was needed. Xerxes, ever the showman, decided to make a big production out of it. So he conducted what today would be called a beauty pageant, the difference being...er...never mind. You will figure it out.

Attractive young virgins were collected from throughout the empire and placed in the royal harem for a year of beauty treatments. After this they were interviewed by the king, so to speak. The winner would become the new queen. The losers became concubines.

Pause here. This scene also grates on modern sensibilities. *How demeaning to women!* You may consider the ancients to have been barbaric and oppressive. I will only say that it is too easy sport to sit in judgement on other cultures. You may correctly see the speck in their eye but be unaware of the log in yours, as Jesus would describe it.

In any case, the queen vacancy was viewed as opportunity not oppression. Who wouldn't jump at a chance at royalty? Even the consolation prize was not bad. Life in the harem would be an improvement for many of the women. No doubt their lives could have been better. But they could also have been worse.

The biblical text does not tell us why Esther became a contestant, only that she did. It does tell us that she excelled in her circumstances. Like Joseph and Daniel, she made quite a good impression on her superiors.

> Now Esther was winning favor in the eyes of all who saw her.
>
> Esther 2:15

Especially Xerxes.

> The king loved Esther more than all the women, and she won grace and favor in his sight more than all the virgins, so that he set the royal crown on her head and made her queen instead of Vashti.
>
> Esther 2:17

As was his way, Xerxes throws another party celebrating the new queen and proclaiming a holiday in her honor.

Enter Haman

Now if you want all of the details of this story, you can read it for yourself. I will skip to the part where Esther gets deeply involved in political scheming.

There was a bad guy. Haman. When he is introduced the king had just promoted him above all other court officials. They now were required to "bow down or pay homage" to him as he passed through the city gate. It is easy to imagine this becoming a contest to display the most enthusiasm.

ESTHER

This is called "kissing up" in the vernacular, a common practice among the aspiring in the civil service.

But one fellow did not participate. Mordecai. He was a Jew. Just as importantly, he was Esther's cousin—a father figure to her actually, since her parents had died and Mordecai had adopted her. If you are paying attention here, you would have figured out that Esther too was a Jew, a fact that Mordecai had told her to keep to herself.

Haman was the vindictive type. He wanted Mordecai dead. Better yet, why not kill all of the Jews. Genocide. The final solution. So he sold it to the king, using some of the same techniques as Daniel's enemies.

> There is a certain people scattered abroad and dispersed among the peoples in all the provinces of your kingdom. Their laws are different from those of every other people, and they do not keep the king's laws, so that it is not to the king's profit to tolerate them. If it please the king, let it be decreed that they be destroyed, and I will pay 10,000 talents of silver into the hands of those who have charge of the king's business, that they may put it into the king's treasuries."
>
> Esther 3:8-9

To summarize: 1) there is this subversive group of people, unnamed of course; 2) they are lawbreakers, no mention of laws broken; and 3) the royal treasury will be enriched, analysis of greater economic impact lacking.

Xerxes' response.

> The money is given to you, the people also, to do with them as it seems good to you.
>
> Esther 3:11

The character sketch that is forming of the king is not flattering. He was a party animal. He was not a good judge of character, e.g. Haman. He was loose with government money. And most importantly, he was easily manipulated.

Esther knew all of this. And she shrewdly exploited the last trait to counter the evil that Haman intended.

But I jump ahead.

The Crisis Response Team

Mordecai exchanged his wardrobe for sackcloth and ashes and wandered about the city crying bitterly, as other Jews were doing. Esther heard of his actions and sent one of her minions to find out why he was behaving so.

Although the entire city was aware of the decree, Esther evidently was not. This is interesting. She was queen, but she was not politically connected...or even politically informed. The royal women were to be seen—as eye candy, apparently—but not heard when it came to matters of state.

Mordecai commanded her "to go to the king to beg his favor and plead with him on behalf of her people." But she responded with a point of law. No one could approach the king without being summoned. The penalty was death...unless the king extended his scepter. Furthermore, Esther had not seen him in a month.

Mordecai warned that she would not escape the death sentence. And then delivered this well-known speech.

> For if you keep silent at this time, relief and deliverance will rise for the Jews from another place, but you and your father's house will perish. And who knows whether you have not come to the kingdom for such a time as this?
>
> Esther 4:14

He ended with that famous rhetorical question. "Who knows whether you have not come to the kingdom for such a time as this?" God knew, of course. He had sovereignly placed Esther there as certainly as he has placed you in your circumstances within the kingdom of the world.

Esther agreed to approach the king and asked for prayer. And then uttered the best line in the book. "If I perish, I perish."

You know the rest of the story. Esther fearlessly stormed into the throne room and demanded that her husband find some loophole to rescue the Jews. Xerxes, as was his manner, becomes enraged and has her head removed on the spot. (These sassy queens were becoming wearisome to him.) The Jews were slaughtered. And Esther becomes one of the most beloved heroines of the ages.

Huh? That's not the way I remember it.

Okay. I changed the ending. The real story reveals a great deal more political savvy on Esther's part.

Xerxes extends the scepter and...wait for it...Esther invites the king and Haman to lunch. They go. *These palace games are so fun.* What does she really want? She wants...wait for it...them to come to another feast the next day. Then she will reveal her request.

Now it just so happened (reminder: this is code for God's rule within the everlasting kingdom) that Xerxes could not sleep that night. So he ordered some lackey to bring in the book of memorable deeds and read it to him. What would end insomnia better than a few pages of the royal chronicles? It turns out that Mordecai had uncovered an assassination plot against the king and saved his life. And what did he get for this faithful service to the crown? Nothing.

Xerxes was still thinking about this the next day. Enter Haman, who came to ask permission to hang the king's protector. Before he got the chance, Xerxes asked him what should be done for the man he wants to honor. Haman assumes that "the man" was himself, of course. So he came up with the idea of a parade. The king thinks that is pretty good and orders Haman to do so for Mordecai.

This turn of events upsets Haman and he runs home to whine about it. But not for long. He is rushed off to the Esther's second banquet.

Now comes the climax. The moment is finally right to plead for her life and for all of the Jews. (Timing is everything in politics.) And so she made her case. Xerxes asked who would do such a thing? Well, duh! It was Haman, that vile excuse for a man.

The king, always one to react with unbridled emotion, flew into a rage. Haman begs Esther for mercy and in his distress invades her personal space, which only made matters worse for him.

Epilogue

Haman swung from the gallows. Esther received Haman's estate. Mordecai advanced into Haman's position.

Esther, in tears, again begged the king for the deliverance of her people. This was the second time she risked her life to approach the throne without being summoned. Xerxes once more extended the scepter.

She asked him to "to revoke the letters devised by Haman." The king's answer was twofold. First, he reiterated that he had given her Haman's property and had hung the rascal. Second, Mordecai was directed to clean up the Jewish issue.

> But you may write as you please with regard to the Jews, in the name of the king, and seal it with the king's ring, for an edict written in the name of the king and sealed with the king's ring cannot be revoked.
>
> Esther 8:8

Did you pay attention to the last part of the sentence? "…for an edict written in the name of the king and sealed with the king's ring cannot be revoked." Apparently Esther did not recall this bit of law, which even you should be aware of from the last chapter. She had asked for the Jewish purge to be cancelled, but it could not be undone.

I criticize Esther here, but only very mildly. This was not her area of expertise. Her contribution was to maneuver the king, which she accomplished with great courage, wit and wile. But she could not do everything. Nobody ever can. Another was needed.

That would be Mordecai, who had the legal and bureaucratic chops to finish the job. He sent out letters that allowed the Jews to protect themselves and destroy their enemies, which they did. And who knows whether Mordecai had not come to the kingdom for such a time as this?

* * *

Everything you despise about politics in the kingdom of the world is in the little book of Esther, isn't it? Scheming. Misdirection. Manipulation. What may surprise you is that these tactics can be used not only for evil but also for good.

19 Paul

The Book of Acts
1st Century AD

The Apostle Paul is known for his missionary journeys, his evangelism, church planting and, of course, his writings. His instruction on government in Romans chapter thirteen is the most definitive in the Bible. But our focus is now on demonstration not instruction. How did Paul practice what he preached?

And one more thing about our subject. Unlike the others I have highlighted so far, Paul was not within the ruling structure of government. He was not even a minor functionary within the bureaucracy.

This is not to say that he had no political power. I have made the case that both ruler and ruled possess political power. And, as you shall see, Paul was a master of using the system to accomplish a good purpose.

Illegalities

About half of the book of Acts is focused on Paul. I suppose I could have sifted through all of this and expounded upon his politics in comprehensive detail. But I am far too lazy for such monotonous work. Instead, I will zoom in on the most significant passages.

First to Philippi, a Macedonian city. Paul and company were evangelizing there and a slave girl possessed by a demon followed them around for days yelling at them. This hindered their work, as you can imagine it would yours. Paul finally had enough and cast the demon out of the girl.

You would think that this would universally be recognized as a good thing. But no. The demon enabled the girl to tell fortunes, evidently a very profitable business. Her owners realized that their revenue stream had suddenly dried up, so they hauled Paul and Silas before the civil authorities and laid out charges.

> We have been exploiting this poor little slave girl and now we can't anymore. Make these Jews put the demon back in her!

Did you fall for that? I hope not. Just another of my shameless distortions to make a point. Here is what they actually said.

> These men are Jews, and they are disturbing our city. They advocate customs that are not lawful for us as Romans to accept or practice.
> Acts 16:20-21

Very clever of them. They changed what should have been a civil suit (loss of future business revenue) into a criminal suit (disturbing the peace and law breaking). They topped it off with their status as Roman citizens. They were the people that mattered to the magistrates, not some rabble-rousing outsiders.

Well, that seemed to do the trick. Paul and Silas were stripped, beaten and thrown into prison.

What follows is a wonderful account of the salvation of the jailer and his family, plus Paul and Silas' miraculous deliverance from prison. But I must avoid these uplifting excursions in order to stay focused on politics.

In the morning the magistrates sent the order to release Paul and Silas. The jailer conveyed this message and added his own blessing, "Go in peace." You would think that would be the end of the legal matter. A beating. A night in jail. The sentence served and completed. But no. Paul would not let it go.

> They have beaten us publicly, uncondemned, men who are Roman citizens, and have thrown us into prison; and do they now throw us out secretly? No! Let them come themselves and take us out.
> Acts 16:37

This is not the approach I would have taken. *If you're good, I'm good. I'm outta here!* But Paul talked law. The rules had been broken...by the magistrates. Why? Because Paul and Silas were Roman citizens. Roman citizen had rights and they had been violated.

The last sentence is the most interesting of all. "Let them come themselves and take us out." What was the purpose of demanding an escort out of jail by the rulers? It publically declared that Paul and Silas had been treated unjustly. This was no doubt humiliating to the magistrates. But better to be humiliated than to suffer the consequences if Paul and Silas pressed charges against them.

More importantly, it protected the new believers in Philippi. Why? Because the illegal actions of the rulers could be raised again if the believers were persecuted. To emphasize the point, Paul and Silas met with the Christians before leaving town.

Politics are a power sport. For both rulers and the ruled.

Riot!

Next I would like to highlight a series of events and government interactions. The first scene occurs in Jerusalem. Paul had just arrived and the leaders of the church warned him of Jewish opposition. They said that Paul had been teaching Jews not to circumcise their children and practice other customs of Moses' law. The church leaders asked Paul to observe certain purification rites in order to publically demonstrate his practice of Jewish customs. This he did.

The trouble began when he was at the temple. His enemies recognized him and repeated their rumors. They added that he had brought Greeks into the temple area, defiling it.

Accusations do not have to be true to be effective. These were very effective. The crowd at the temple turned into an angry mob, which soon grew into a riot throughout the city. Paul was the center of their attention. They were trying to kill him.

The Roman tribune was informed of the situation. This was a problem for him. Why? Because his job was to maintain order. Order is the primary responsibility of all civil rulers. But order had suddenly broken down. If he did not quickly restore it, things would go from bad to worse. And he would be in big trouble with the Roman higher ups.

So he took his troops and arrested Paul and bound him in chains. The tribune asked Paul what he had done, but the crowd noise did not allow for conversation. When the troops had carried Paul to the safety of the military barracks, he was able to speak to the tribune.

> May I [Paul] say something to you? ...I am a Jew, from Tarsus in Cilicia, a citizen of no obscure city. I beg you, permit me to speak to the people.
>
> Acts 21:37, 39

Now if I have influenced you at all, you should have noticed something here.

I see it. Paul identifies himself as a Roman citizen.

Very good. Perhaps my labors on this book will not be a waste of time after all.

Paul, who now had the rapt attention of a large audience, gave his conversion testimony and rebutted the charges against him at the same time. It all seemed to be going well until he mentioned something about the Gentiles, a controversial topic with Jews. Pandemonium once again ensued.

The tribune ordered Paul to be taken inside the barracks to be flogged and questioned. This is a tried and true technique of law enforcement—flog and question, although it has fallen out of favor in some places nowadays.

As the story goes, when they had prepared Paul for flogging, he gets the attention of a nearby officer.

> **Is it lawful for you to flog a man who is a Roman citizen and uncondemned?**
>
> Acts 22:25

If you have been keeping count, this is the third time Paul has played his citizenship card. The first time in Philippi he played it after he was beaten. Now he has played it twice before he was beaten. This—it seems to me—is the preferred timing.

Paul is the one who wrote, "But our citizenship is in heaven...."[17] Of course it is! A Christian is a citizen of the spiritual kingdom of God. But you are also a citizen of the kingdom of the world. Paul knew this and used it repeatedly to advance the Gospel. So should you.

To return to the action, the officer reported Paul's citizenship claim to the tribune, who should have remembered Paul telling him this directly a few paragraphs ago. But such details are often forgotten during these hectic emergencies that pop up now and again. In any case, the message had been fully received now.

The tribune was "afraid." This was understandable. He had illegally bound a Roman citizen in chains. However, there is no hint in the text that Paul threatened to press the issue as he did with the Philippian magistrates. Why? Because the tribune was his protector, not his tormentor. A political move that is appropriate in one situation may not wise in another.

The tribune held Paul's life in his hands, as you shall see. Best to keep in his good graces.

---

[17] See Philippines 3:20.

PAUL

The Trials of Palace Life

Scene two. The next day the tribune arranged for Paul to face his accusers. To cut to the chase, this resulted in a heated debate between the Sadducees and the Pharisees. The Jewish leaders—realizing that Paul had outmaneuvered them—decided that they would kill him.

A drastic tactic. An illegal one too.

Now it just so happened that Paul's nephew overheard the plot. He told Paul and Paul told him to tell the tribune, which he did. The tribune then sent Paul under military escort to Governor Felix at Caesarea.

This effectively placed the burden of ruling in this matter on the governor's back. After all, the tribune didn't have any idea what all of these Jews were squabbling about. Didn't know. Didn't want to know. Way above his pay grade.

Scene three. Five days later the Jewish leaders and their lawyer arrived in Caesarea to press their case against Paul. The lawyer spoke first. But our interest is not in his cunning and oily speech. We want to know how Paul conducted himself. Here are a few excerpts from what he said.

> Knowing that for many years you have been a judge over this nation, I cheerfully make my defense. You can verify that it is not more than twelve days since I went up to worship in Jerusalem, and they did not find me disputing with anyone or stirring up a crowd…. But this I confess to you, that according to the Way, which they call a sect, I worship the God of our fathers, believing everything laid down by the Law and written in the Prophets, having a hope in God, which these men themselves accept, that there will be a resurrection of both the just and the unjust. So I always take pains to have a clear conscience toward both God and man.
>
> Acts 24:10-16

A few observations. Paul was respectful to the ruler, as he has instructed you to be. He defended himself against unjust and untrue charges. And he wove his personal testimony into the narrative in order to present the Gospel.

If you look underneath Paul's words you will see that they rest upon his understanding of the kingdoms. He was confident that God is sovereign over his everlasting kingdom and is working through all things to accomplish his purposes. He embraced his role in the kingdom of the world and used his political power to defend himself and others against injustice. And his overall objective was to advance the kingdom of God and to defeat the kingdom of Satan.

Paul wove the threads of all four kingdoms into his defense. This is the way he viewed life. Integrated. Just as you should.

Playing by the Rules

Scene Four. Continuing dialog with Felix.

> He [Felix] sent for Paul and heard him speak about faith in Christ Jesus. And as he reasoned about righteousness and self-control and the coming judgment, Felix was alarmed and said, "Go away for the present. When I get an opportunity I will summon you." At the same time he hoped that money would be given him by Paul. So he sent for him often and conversed with him.
>
> Acts 24:24-26

Paul continued to describe spiritual realities to Felix at every opportunity and encouraged him to respond in faith. The governor, however, had another objective. He wanted a bribe.

Hmmm. What to do? Slide some bills under the table? You do something for me. I do something for you. *Quid pro quo*. That's the way it works in the real world, so they say. And besides, wouldn't it accomplish a good purpose—obtain the apostle's release so that he could further the kingdom?

But Paul would not participate in bribery. Bribery is sin. Bribery would have corrupted justice, discredited the church and dishonored Jesus. And do you really think that the God who rules over all would bless behavior that violates his righteousness? I think not.

When you play in politics, you are expected to play by the rules. Playing by the rules, of course, may be a slow process. Two years passed.

Using the Law

Scene Five. Felix was replaced by Festus. The Jewish leaders asked Festus to transfer Paul to Jerusalem. They intended to kill Paul in transit. They were up to their old tricks.

But Festus scheduled a court hearing in Caesarea. The Jews again threw everything they could think of at Paul, none of which they could prove. Paul claimed that he had not violated Moses' law or the temple. And he had done nothing against the Roman government, that is, Caesar. Festus then asked Paul if he was willing to stand trial in Jerusalem.

Now comes a twist in the plot that is unexpected.

> I am standing before Caesar's tribunal, where I ought to be tried. To the Jews I have done no wrong, as you yourself know very well. If then I am a wrongdoer and have committed anything for which I deserve to die, I do not seek to escape death. But if there is nothing to their charges against me, no one can give me up to them. I appeal to Caesar.
>
> Acts 25:10-11

Perhaps Paul knew of the plot to kill him. Perhaps he tired of being stuck in the gears of the legal system. Perhaps this was his opportunity to testify in Rome, as the Lord had revealed to him.[18] Whatever the reason, Paul refused to be turned over to the Jews, who wanted to settle the matter on their terms. To avoid this, he exercised the ultimate right of every Roman citizen—to be tried directly in Caesar's court.

Also note Paul's endorsement of government authority. "If then I am a wrongdoer and have committed anything for which I deserve to die, I do not seek to escape death." Paul submitted himself to the government rules even if that would result in his execution. At the same time, however, he demanded justice from the ruler, which was his right before man and God.

Scene Six. A few days later King Agrippa, ruler of adjacent territory, arrived in Caesarea to welcome Festus to town. Courtesy call. Networking. No telling when the assistance of a brother ruler may be needed to help with all of these restless and troublesome Jews.

I will not summarize Paul's defense before Festus and Agrippa. It follows the same line as his defense before Felix, although tailored to the backgrounds and understanding of the new personalities.

Afterward, they discussed the matter.

> "This man is doing nothing to deserve death or imprisonment." And Agrippa said to Festus, "This man could have been set free if he had not appealed to Caesar."
>
> Acts 26:31-32

There is a bit of irony here. An innocent man remained a Roman prisoner in order to be protected by a pagan state from fellow Jews who intended to kill him. Then again, there is much irony in politics.

---

[18] See Acts 23:11.

* * *

Paul's historical narrative ends in the last chapter of Acts. He is under house arrest awaiting trial. Here too I will end my observations.

The apostle provides an extensive example of godly practice in a fallen world. The situation was complex in his day, just as it is in ours. Through it all, Paul shrewdly leveraged his political power to advance the kingdom of God.

20 William Wilberforce

1759-1833 AD

You may have noticed that there is no Wilberforce in the Bible. If you doubt this, take a minute or two to conduct a word search. No Wilberforce, as I said. He is, however, a well-known figure in history, as is the fellow in the next and last chapter of my biographical survey.

I have selected these two to further my argument for political involvement. The first illustrates patient and persevering government service. The second to…well…it's complicated and I had better not get started on that now.

But I have another reason for including them. Kingdom history is still being written, although it is not being recorded in the Bible. There is much to learn from faithful Christians throughout the last two thousand years.

Dominion Decision

William Wilberforce lived during a time of turbulent change and cultural deterioration in Britain. The social order was debased by widespread prostitution, adultery, corruption, exploitation and drunkenness. While many promoted these "freedoms," Wilberforce pushed against them both personally and politically. He championed a long list of causes.

The one he is most remembered for, of course, is slavery. Against this he waged a long war, taking aim first at the slave trade and then at the abolition of slavery itself.

Wilberforce lost more battles than he won along the way. He knew when to advance and when to retreat. He picked his fights, choosing achievable ones that would eventually succeed instead of grand ones that would end in glorious defeat. When attacked and ridiculed, he remained pleasant and winsome, which was essential to his influence. And he joined with others dedicated to the cause, who had the skills that he lacked. He played a lead role but not the only role.

There is so much to say about this man…but since others have already said it, read their books.

I will, however, highlight one key decision in his life. This occurred shortly after he decided to believe the Gospel about Jesus—his conversion, in the vernacular. He was enthusiastic about his faith, as is the case with all who grasp the grace of God. So the question arose, how should he spend the rest of his life? He had been a member of parliament for five years and was a rising star. But he was willing to give it all up.

He seriously considered withdrawing from political involvement. Perhaps he thought that living a life fully dedicated to God required withdrawing from his "worldly" dominion responsibilities. I have been arguing against this idea throughout this book. The reason I keep digging at it is because its roots are so deep. Perhaps they have crept into your thinking. *If I really want to dedicate my life to God, I had better serve him in a full-time "Christian" vocation. Anything less is wasting my life.* Being a pastor or a missionary may be the role you are gifted for. But these are not the jobs for most of us. For one thing, the rest of us have to pay for them. For another, we are better suited to serve and honor God through other work in the kingdom of the world.

Back to Wilberforce. It just so happened that he asked for counsel from two men. The first was his good friend William Pitt, prime minister at the time. The second was an older man. John Newton—the former slaver and writer of the famous hymn *Amazing Grace*.

These men were very different in many ways, but they gave essentially the same advice. Duty to God included duty to man. Wilberforce should continue in public service.

He did. And the rest is history.

In the Hearts of His Countrymen

The most fitting tribute to Wilberforce's political work is found in words chiseled into a stone monument that resides in Westminster Abbey in London.

I urge you to read it carefully. Politics often leaves its participants bloodied, broken, discarded and forgotten. Often…but not always. All of God's faithful servants will certainly receive their reward in the next world, but some also gain recognition in this one.

WILLIAM WILBERFORCE

To the memory of William Wilberforce
(born in Hull, August 24th 1759, died in London, July 29th 1833)

For nearly half a century a member of the House of Commons,
and, for six parliaments during that period,
one of the two representatives for Yorkshire.

In an age and country fertile in great and good men,
he was among the foremost of those who fixed the
character of their times;
because to high and various talents,
to warm benevolence, and to universal candour,
he added the abiding eloquence of a Christian life.

Eminent as he was in every department of public labour,
and a leader in every work of charity,
whether to relieve the temporal or the spiritual wants of his fellow-men,
his name will ever be specially identified with those exertions which,
by the blessing of God, removed from England
the guilt of the African slave trade,
and prepared the way for the abolition of slavery
in every colony of the empire:

In the prosecution of these objects he relied,
not in vain, on God;
but in the progress he was called to endure
great obloquy and great opposition:
he outlived, however, all enmity;
and in the evening of his days,
withdrew from public life and public observation
to the bosom of his family.
Yet he died not unnoticed or forgotten by his country:
the Peers and Commons of England,
with the Lord Chancellor and the Speaker at their head,
in solemn procession from their respective houses,
carried him to his fitting place
among the mighty dead around, here to repose:
till, through the merits of Jesus Christ,
his only redeemer and saviour,
(whom, in his life and in his writings he had desired to glorify,)
he shall rise in the resurrection of the just.

21 Dietrich Bonhoeffer

1906-1945 AD

I have dreaded writing this chapter about Dietrich Bonhoeffer, the well-known German theologian and pastor that opposed Hitler and was executed for it.

What's the problem?

Well…everyone else that I have highlighted worked within their existing political structures, flawed as they were. That is, everyone else more or less followed the rules. The only exceptions being when the rules directly and blatantly required them to violate God's higher standards or commands.

But Bonhoeffer worked to remove and replace the existing government. Even more challenging is the fact that he was involved in a plot to assassinate the ruler of that government.

This raises the question of limits and boundaries. How far can you go to resist injustice?

Pacifism

Bonhoeffer was not a person you would suspect of being involved in a conspiracy to overthrow the government. Why do I say that? Because I read his book *The Cost of Discipleship*. Here is one passage that is representative of a theme throughout the book.

> The followers of Jesus have been called to peace. …And to that end they renounce all violence and tumult. In the cause of Christ nothing is to be gained by such methods. …His disciples keep the peace by choosing to endure suffering themselves rather than inflict it on others.

> ...They renounce all self-assertion, and quietly suffer in the face of hatred and wrong. In so doing they overcome evil with good, and establish the peace of God in the midst of a world of war and hate.[19]

He first published *The Cost of Discipleship* in 1937, four years into Hitler's rule. Although the full extent of Hitler's program was not known at this point, there was no doubt that it was evil and had already done great harm.

Bonhoeffer resisted that evil but only by non-violent political means. From the beginning of Nazi influence he had opposed the persecution of the Jews, the corruption of the church, and many other expressions of evil.

The church situation in Germany during Nazi rule (1933-45) was complex. In general, Hitler exploited the church-state relationship to obtain support for Nazi ideology. In this he was largely—although not completely—successful.

But my focus is not on the response of the institutional church—how this systematically occurred or how the church should have resisted or the theological and social reasons the church capitulated. My focus is on the political response of the individual, that is, on Bonhoeffer's response.

At first Bonhoeffer was a pacifist. And then he wasn't.

What changed?

Not Pacifism

All attempts to resist and reverse Hitler's influence were failing. Everything was getting worse and worse. The church was largely compromised. The Jews were being annihilated. And it was thought that Christian civilization itself hung in the balance.

At what point Bonhoeffer joined the resistance is unknown. In fact, much is unknown about his rationale and involvement. Why? Because when you are involved in a conspiracy against a totalitarian state, it is not prudent to talk about it, much less to openly write about it. To do so would endanger yourself and other conspirators.

Yet Bonhoeffer does give some hints in what he was able to write. And those who knew him have shared their thoughts about his motives. Their opinions in this matter are certainly better than mine. Here, for example, is what his brother-in-law Gerhard Leibholz said in the forward to my edition of *The Cost of Discipleship*.

---

[19] Dietrich Bonhoeffer, *The Cost of Discipleship*, (New York: The Macmillan Company, 1963), 126.

> In the earlier stages of his career Bonhoeffer accepted the traditional Lutheran view that there was a sharp distinction between politics and religion. Gradually, however, he revised his opinion, not because he was a politician or because he refused to give Caesar his due, but because he came to recognize that the political authority in Germany had become entirely corrupt and immoral and that a false faith is capable of terrible and monstrous things. For Bonhoeffer Hitler was the Antichrist, the arch-destroyer of the world and its basic values, the Antichrist who enjoys destruction, slavery, death and extinction for their own sake, the Antichrist who wants to pose the negative as positive and as creative. Bonhoeffer was firmly and rightly convinced that it is not only a Christian right but a Christian duty towards God to oppose tyranny, that is, a government which is no longer based on natural law and the law of God.[20]

The question for us is not if we should oppose tyranny. The question is how we should oppose tyranny. What means are consistent with God's commands?

Apparently Bonhoeffer struggled greatly with this question and never fully resolved it in his own mind. As is often the case with politics, he was forced to choose between acting and not acting. The consequences were severe either way.

Bonhoeffer chose conspiracy and assassination. If he was wrong, he trusted that God would forgive him. He thought the greater sin would be not to take extreme actions and let the evil continue.

Ponderation

There is much to consider whenever rebellion against government is contemplated. I will list some of them, in no particular order.

- Biblical commands require general obedience to rulers, although not absolute obedience. Therefore, disobedience in whatever form should only be a last resort after all means within the rules have failed.

---

[20] Ibid., 30.

- The assassination of a ruler is the most extreme of all political actions. Only an extraordinarily evil ruler and unjust rules warrant consideration of such a course. In almost all cases it is better to follow David's example, who refused to kill Saul even after God providentially delivered Saul into his hands.

- Murder (i.e. unjust killing) is always sin but not all killing is murder. Killing under the authority of the state to punish the murderer, to ensure civil order, and to defend against foreign aggressors is generally considered to be just.

- An individual should be permitted to defend himself or others when threatened unjustly with harm. If the only means to do so is deadly force, then the killing is justified.

- However, when an individual considers the government to be unjust and "takes matters into his own hands" by assassination or other acts of mayhem, this person is rightly considered a madman or a terrorist and is subject to the punishment of the state.

- Citizens may join together in order to remove an unjust government and establish a more just one. Those involved may be characterized as either traitors and rebels or as patriots and heroes, depending upon the sympathies of those writing the history.

- Rebellion (or liberation, if you prefer) by definition brings about civil disorder, usually involving death and destruction. It should, therefore, never be attempted without some expectation of success. But the more desperate the situation, the more motivation for the attempt—no matter how desperate.

That's enough of your on-the-one-hand-this and on-the-other-hand-that blathering. Commit! Make up your mind! Was Bonhoeffer right or wrong to join the conspiracy to assassinate Hitler?

Er...

I can't believe you're waffling on this. You've got an opinion on everything else.

THE KINGDOM OF THE WORLD

Okay...take another example. The American Revolution—right or wrong?

Pick Your Battles

Instead of answering, I'll ask some questions of my own. What level of injustice justifies the ruled to break the rules and resist the rulers? What extent of resistance is allowed? And how and when do you promote justice?

You would like some clear rules to define this game. So would I! As for Bonhoeffer, I am not going to judge him. Jesus will do that. I am content to let the Lord sort this out. It is his job, not mine.

If you think about it, though, his case is an extreme example of a political decision. You are surrounded by lesser decisions all of the time. When you vote, for example, you must weigh many factors, both positive and negative. Add to that the multitude of everyday choices you make either as ruler or ruled.

Furthermore, your political actions are shaped to an extent by your abilities, interests and influences. These should drive what battles you choose to fight. You cannot fight them all. Nobody can.

Your duty may be on the local school board. Or maybe you should run for congress. Or write letters to the editor. Or blog. Or...whatever.

My role, I think, is to sit comfortably and safely at my little desk and contemplate the "big picture." You may think that I am all talk and no action. True enough. Your battle may be in the arena. For you it is blood, sweat and tears. My battle occurs mostly inside my head. *I wonder how many kingdoms there are? Why do hermits reject their dominion responsibilities? Should I drink another cup of coffee?*

The point is, I have my place. You have yours.

The best advice I can give is to ask God for wisdom. And given all the difficulties of life, never do something you are convinced is wrong. As Martin Luther said, "To go against conscience is neither right nor safe."

Speaking of conscience, this is a topic that requires further examination. But first, I must wrap up this section of the book.

Uh...what about the American Revolution?

22 Lessons Learned

So, do you think that these biographies validated the Dominion Mandate and kingdom concepts I described in Part I of this book?

Maybe…I'm still chewing on that. But I was hoping that you would provide some more definitive guidelines that would help me make political decisions. Instead, you seem to be saying that one principle may apply here but another there. And you topped it all off at the end of the last chapter by saying that I need to figure out it on my own anyway!

You are understanding me correctly. I do not like checklists. The problem with them is that they never account for all of the complexities and nuances that you actually face. Life in a four-kingdom reality does not lend itself to such simplicity.

Wise Solomon knew this. See how he instructs, for example, on responding to a fool.

> Answer not a fool according to his folly, lest you be like him yourself.
>
> Answer a fool according to his folly, lest he be wise in his own eyes.
>
> Proverbs 26:4-5

Sometimes you should answer him. Sometimes not. Life is tough that way. So is politics. I am willing, however, to summarize a few general observations from the lives of those I have surveyed.

All Different…But the Same

I'll begin with the fascinating variety of political structures we encountered. Here they are in order

Joseph – Egypt under Pharaoh
Boaz – Israel during the Judges
Obadiah – Northern Kingdom of Israel under Ahab
Jonah – Nineveh, Assyria
Daniel – Babylon/Medes and Persians
Esther – Persian Royal Court
Paul – Roman Empire
Wilberforce – 19th Century Britain
Bonhoeffer – Nazi Germany

While these kingdoms of the world were all very different from one another in many ways, they were alike in one aspect. They were spiritual battlegrounds between good and evil. Some people attempted to use the institution of government for evil. Others for good. Depending upon their spiritual allegiance.

God requires you to pull toward what is good and push against what is evil, whether you are the ruler or the ruled. Both roles contain political power and each has its responsibilities. The rulers are to rule righteously. The ruled are to submit to the rulers.

But there are exceptions. Submission is a general command not an absolute command. The people I examined only refused to comply with a few specific rules not all rules. That may be surprising considering the governments in question. Take another look at the list above. None of them were completely pure. Actually, none of them were even close. (Just as the government you are under includes much injustice.) Yet godly people served in them with distinction.

The danger in acknowledging exceptions to obedience is that some people may too easily use this to justify disobedience to or even rebellion against a government. Be careful with that! Every government is a mixture of good and evil rules. Some evil does not make all evil. Disobedience and rebellion destroy the civil order, which is business you should avoid if at all possible. Your objective is peace not chaos.

You will need patience in most of your political pursuits. While there are historical examples of rapid change, politics are usually painfully incremental. Two steps forward. One step back. Perhaps two or three steps back. Failure typically precedes success. And within the everlasting kingdom, God's sovereign plan may include your political failure…or perhaps success in a way you will not see. Be content with that. God knows more than you do.

Don't try to fix all that is wrong. That is impossible. To attempt everything ends up accomplishing nothing. Aim at specific targets—ones that are suited to your particular interests and strengths. Pick and choose.

LESSONS LEARNED

And finally, one more thing. Review the list of people above. Think about their lives. Were they defined only by what they did or also by who they were? Accomplishment or character? Both, of course. God was not only at work through them. Just as importantly—or perhaps more importantly—he was at work in them. Politics just happened to be the means he used to shape and form them. Did they obey God? Did they remain faithful to him? Will you? Nothing is more significant in the kingdom of God.

Justice and the Kingdom
Part III

In the first section of this book I described the kingdom of the world as it has been since the fall of man and will be until the return of King Jesus. The Dominion Mandate and the four kingdoms are the context for all of human history, including politics, during this age. In the second section I told the stories of various political actors. You probably had not viewed most of them from this perspective before, and I hope they illustrate the complexities of striving for good in the kingdom of the world. In the third and final section of the book I will focus on the particular challenges to your political dominion role posed by contemporary culture. By "contemporary" I refer not to the latest 24-hour news cycle but to the influences of the last one hundred years or so that have shaped today's political discourse.

This discourse is always in the context of justice. Which is a good thing. Justice is what is morally right and fair. It is the goal of good civil order. And it is so universally esteemed that the core of every political argument is an appeal for justice.

EVERY ONE.

Why is that?

It is because mankind bears the image of God, regardless of beliefs that may be to the contrary. And because of this, people long for justice. This is an evidence of biblical teaching concerning the spiritual aspect of man and his accountability to the God who created him.

The problem is not that there is so much justice talk but that even the most destructive and wicked of politics are wrapped in it. Someone is lying about justice and others are believing the lies. Even the liar is often so immersed in the lies that he believes them himself. The result? Good is seen as evil and evil as good. Satan's kingdom scores a victory. But truth may win too. And when it does, the kingdom of God advances on earth as it is in heaven.

An understanding of justice is inseparable from three related concepts. Religion, love and law. I will describe how the distortion of each of these corrupts the practice of justice. But first I must delve deeper into the very being of man. And to help me do that, I will enlist a clever little cricket.

23 Conscience and Justice

Jiminy Cricket was Pinoccio's conscience in the classic 1940 Disney movie. In case you are so old that you have forgotten or so young that you never knew the story, let me recap.

Old Gepetto carves a wooden marionette and wishes that he were a real boy not just a puppet. Enter the Blue Fairy, who brings Pinoccio to life. But she will only make him fully human, flesh and blood, if he proves himself brave, truthful and unselfish. To assist him in this task, Jiminy is to advise him on what is right and what is wrong.

To celebrate the situation, the cricket breaks out in song: "When you get in trouble and you don't know right from wrong…when you meet temptation and the urge is very strong…take the straight and narrow path and if you start to slide…always let your conscience be your guide."

Well, as the story goes, Pinoccio does not listen to his conscience and gets into plenty of trouble. He even lies to the Blue Fairy, who warns him that "a boy who won't be good might just as well be made of wood." In the end, though, Pinoccio proves himself brave, truthful and unselfish and becomes a real boy.

That is good stuff.

Is there some connection between a cartoon about a cricket and politics?

Focus on the moral teaching. Conscience is your inner voice, your sense of right and wrong, your guide in ethical matters.

But enough of crickets. Let's move on to the Bible.

The Heart of the Matter

Scripture has much to say about conscience.

You should first recognize its presence in the Garden of Eden. Adam and Eve hid from God after they sinned against him. Why? Because they knew that they had done wrong. How did they know? Conscience. And since they were equipped with conscience, so were all of their descendants. The entire human race. Every one of us.

Conscience is not explained in the Old Testament. It is simply assumed. It is included in what is figuratively called the "heart," which is the broader term used for the inner man in both Testaments. Heart is the non-material aspect of man. It is the source of thoughts, passions, desires, appetites, motivations, affections, reasoning, understanding and faith.

In the following passage, the effect of conscience is clearly seen in David's life.

> But David's **heart struck him** after he had numbered the people. And David said to the LORD, "I have sinned greatly in what I have done."
> II Samuel 24:10

David's conscience spoke. He listened. Unfortunately, not everyone does.

> But Pharaoh **hardened his heart** this time also, and did not let the people go.
> Exodus 8:32

Pharaoh ignored his conscience and rebelled against God. As a result, his heart hardened. Pharaoh continued along this line becoming more and more stiff necked (a biblical metaphor) and block headed (my expression), refusing to submit to God.

Which brings us to the New Testament. The Apostle Paul describes conscience in the book of Romans.

> For the wrath of God is revealed from heaven against all ungodliness and unrighteousness of men, who by their unrighteousness **suppress the truth**. For what can be known about God is **plain to them**, because God has **shown it to them**.
> Romans 1:18-19

People instinctively sense the difference between right and wrong, good and evil. This is the result of being created by God and in his image. In addition to the internal witness of conscience there is the external witness of creation. Look around. It is obvious that there is a God and that he rules over all.

What happens when someone deliberately represses these evidences?

Paul says that God will give them over to "dishonorable passions" and a "debased mind." In their attempt to free themselves from God they enslave themselves to degrading desires.

Up to this point in Romans Paul has included the entire human family in his critique. Then he addresses Jews who think that they are morally superior because they have been given Moses' law. But while this knowledge is a great advantage, God's judgement is solely based on personal righteousness.

> For when Gentiles, who do not have the law, by nature do what the law requires, they are a law to themselves, even though they do not have the law. They show that the work of the law is written on their **hearts**, while their **conscience** also bears witness, and their conflicting thoughts accuse or even excuse them on that day when, according to my gospel, God judges the secrets of men by Christ Jesus.
>
> Romans 2:14-15

Here is the biblical definition of conscience. "The work of the law is written on their hearts." Every person has an internal understanding of morality and justice as a member of the human race, whether or not they are familiar with Scripture and whether or not they submit to it.

But the most amazing revelation in this passage is that conscience will be a witness for the prosecution at the final judgement. Imagine how that might play out!

> Jesus: *And how about the time you took that cookie out of the cookie jar?*
>
> You: *My mommy said I could have one.*
>
> Your Conscience: *Excuse me. She said after dinner not before. For the record, Your Honor, I told him it was stealing and was wrong.*

Back in the here and now, what is the result of violating your conscience? Guilt.

Guilt is painful, unpleasant and disturbing. It is also your friend. "Faithful are the wounds of a friend," as Solomon said. They are for your good. Conscience warns you of danger. It is the spiritual equivalent of your physical nervous system. The latter instructs you to take your hand off of a hot stove. The former tells you when you are harming yourself morally.

And it's not just a personal internal alarm. Conscience does not limit itself to advising you on strictly private matters—the morality of your thoughts. It looks outward as well as inward. It examines public right or wrong. The issues that David and Pharaoh wrestled with in the passages above were in response to their political actions.

So far this conscience business seems pretty simple. Actually, too simple. There is more to the picture.

When Wrong Seems Right

Conscience may be wrong. This seems to contradict what I have been saying. But I am not making it up. I am only trying to convey the full biblical teaching. Blame the Apostle Paul. Not me.

On several occasions Paul boasted that he had always followed his conscience, including this time when he was being examined by the Jewish leaders in Jerusalem.

> And looking intently at the council, Paul said, "Brothers, I have lived my life before God in all **good conscience** up to this day."
>
> Acts 23:1

Paul was following conscience…even when he was a Pharisee in good standing and was persecuting Christians. At the time he thought it was the right thing to do. He thought his actions were consistent with serving God.

> I myself was convinced that I ought to do many things in opposing the name of Jesus of Nazareth. And I did so in Jerusalem. I not only locked up many of the saints in prison after receiving authority from the chief priests, but when they were put to death I cast my vote against them.
>
> Acts 26:9-10

Looking back, though, Paul said that he had "acted ignorantly in unbelief."[21] It was his ignorance about Jesus that had allowed his conscience to support the persecution of Christians. But when he was confronted by the Lord on the road to Damascus his opinion about Jesus was proven false. *Jesus is not a dead cult leader! He is God! Uh-oh!*

His conscience now condemned some actions it had formerly approved. In his first letter to Timothy he described himself as the "foremost" of sinners." That was not a rhetorical embellishment. Paul's persecution of

---

[21] See I Timothy 1:13.

Christians was a painful memory for him.

Fortunately, Paul knew that Jesus could cleanse his conscience and remove his guilt.

> ...how much more will the blood of Christ, who through the eternal Spirit offered himself without blemish to God, purify our **conscience** from dead works to serve the living God.
>
> Hebrews 9:14

But if conscience was created in the image of God and reflects God's standards, how could it be wrong? There must be another influence on conscience.

There is.

It is the lawyers.

The Lawyers

I have been describing conscience as a judge—a judge that provides the heart's moral discernment about beliefs and issues. Now if a judge judges, there must be lawyers lawyering. A judge does not issue a verdict based on nothing. A judge issues a verdict based on the evidence presented by the lawyers and by their arguments to interpret the rules one way or the other.

The lawyers. Who are they? The lawyers represent what is called "worldview" or "ideology" or "philosophy" or "religion." They are the ideas that frame and interpret the information considered by conscience. In short, the lawyers are beliefs.

When I label conscience and beliefs as judge and lawyers, I am using a literary technique called allegory. If that still does not ring a bell, recall Jesus' parables.

I know what allegory is! I told you not to make me look like an idiot!

Just checking.

Here is the thing about lawyers. They have an agenda. They are not neutral or disinterested parties. They do not evenhandedly present facts and ideas from every perspective. They present them from a certain perspective. That perspective may be right or wrong. It may be true or false.

Here is another thing about lawyers. Although there are many lawyers in the world representing the great variety of beliefs, you hire only one. I should say that you hire only one at a time. You may discard some beliefs and adopt others several times during your lifetime. Your current lawyer is the one who presents the arguments inherent in your beliefs to your conscience.

Where does your lawyer come from? He usually comes from the culture that surrounds you. These may be the beliefs held by family, friends, community, teachers, celebrities, rulers, religious leaders or some combination that you have cobbled together. Furthermore, everyone believes that their beliefs are right and that you should believe them too. People want their lawyer to be your lawyer. That is fair enough. I hope you want your lawyer to be their lawyer.

Here is one last thing about lawyers. There is usually one lawyer in a society that is more prominent than any of the others. This lawyer is very influential in shaping public institutions. How can you recognize this lawyer? His beliefs are the ones that are taught and reinforced throughout a culture.

Nowadays this is the atheist's lawyer. And like all lawyers, he attempts to discredit the case of competing lawyers, which means that he is working hard to discredit your biblical beliefs.

Stop!

What's wrong?

You've gotten completely off track with this lawyer allegory. You are driving me crazy! You are supposed to be writing about politics!

I was just about to come to that. Consider all of this a long introduction.

Courtroom Drama

Politics are a contest over whose beliefs will rule and make the rules. Who will succeed in influencing the culture? Who will dominate society? This is a fight that is never settled. There are always competing beliefs jostling for influence. Some may be prominent today. Others tomorrow.

So picture a mob of lawyers punching each other out in a boxing ring....

Now you are mixing metaphors!

I have gotten carried away. Forgive me.

Consider the kingdom of the world in the first century. Judaism existed within the larger Greco-Roman culture imposed throughout the Roman empire. Even within Judaism there were a number of competing political beliefs regarded this ruling culture. There were the Pharisees (*Resist!*), the Sadducees (*Comply!*), the zealots (*Rebel!*), as well as other groups. Many lawyers. And this is the simplistic version.

Now back to Paul. Before he became a Christian and an apostle Paul believed in Judaism, specifically following the teaching of the Pharisees.

This was the lawyer who was the primary persuader of his conscience.

CONSCIENCE AND JUSTICE

Below I illustrate the roles of lawyer and judge in evaluating an issue and presenting a moral verdict to the heart. Conscience—the judge—is represented by the gavel. The lawyer—worldview—is represented by the symbol above. Here is how Paul would have viewed the persecution of Christians, which was a political issue, through his lawyer of Pharisaical Judaism. Begin at the top.

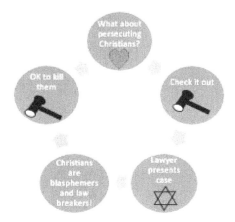

The question here is, "Who are Christians?" But the question behind the question is, "Who is Jesus?" Actually, this is the central and most important question in the universe. In Paul's case, Jesus answered that question in person on the road to Damascus. Result: Paul fired his lawyer for lying about Jesus and hired the one who was telling the truth.[22] Paul now interpreted through the lawyer of Christianity rather than through the lawyer of Judaism.

And what difference did that make? See the revised judgement of conscience concerning the persecution of Christians.

---

[22] Here is an age-old conundrum: Did Paul change his heart because he changed his lawyer? Or did he change his lawyer because he changed his heart? I don't know. I am only trying to describe the functioning within the heart not its timing.

THE KINGDOM OF THE WORLD

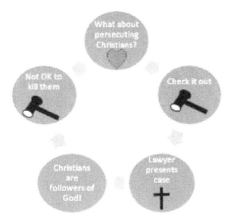

One more observation. Just because conscience makes a ruling does not mean that the heart—the entire inner man—will accept that ruling. Paul could have hardened his heart, ignored the ruling of his conscience and continued his persecution of Christians. Conscience does not dictate to the heart. All the other aspects of the heart may override conscience's judgement and decide guilt is an acceptable price to pay in order to do what it desires to do. In Paul's case, he could have decided that his status and career path within Judaism were too much to forfeit. But that is only speculation, of course. Fortunately, by the grace of God, Paul's heart softened and he listened to conscience.

I have been describing the internal workings of the human heart. It is time now to consider the external spiritual influences.

Spiritual Influences

As they are in every human endeavor, the spiritual kingdoms are present and active in politics. The kingdom of the world is a battleground between the kingdom of God and the kingdom of Satan. These spiritual kingdoms have very different objectives. One is for good. The other for evil. In a political context, one is for justice and the other for injustice.

Think that through. The kingdom of God is for justice because justice is the proper fulfillment of man's responsibility to rule the earth under God. When you rule justly you are submitting to God and reflecting accurately the image of God in you. This glorifies God. This is what you were made to do.

This disgusts the devil. His kingdom foments rebellion against God. How? Well...through every way imaginable. Regarding politics, he does it through injustice to fellow man. Injustice is a perversion of man's rule under God. It is an attack against God by refusing to submit to his rule.

But Satan is a sneaky fellow—the father of lies, a compulsive fibber, a

CONSCIENCE AND JUSTICE

serial deceiver. He does not boldly contradict justice. That would be too obvious. It would set off alarm bells within conscience. Instead, he makes injustice appear to be justice. He makes wrong seem right, just as Paul thought that the persecution of Christians was right.

The kingdom of Satan has an entire propaganda department whose mission is to make lying lawyers seem like truth tellers. This is tricky work. It takes a complex web of distortions and half-truths to disguise the deceptions.

Whereas many in the world may be fooled by these, you are commanded not to be.

> See to it that no one takes you captive by philosophy and empty deceit, according to human tradition, according to the elemental spirits of the world, and not according to Christ.
>
> Colossians 2:8

Once more.

> Do not be conformed to this world,[23] but be transformed by the renewal of your mind, that by testing you may discern what is the will of God, what is good and acceptable and perfect.
>
> Romans 12:2

So make sure your lawyer is biblically informed and pay attention to him.

The Art of Persuasion

And pay attention to the other lawyers too. Why? Because politics are the art of persuasion and you must understand their arguments in order to challenge false beliefs in order to expose their lies.

You may disagree with me on this point.

You may argue that politics are fundamentally about the exercise of power, since government wields the sword and politics wields the governmental hand that wields the sword. True enough. But rulers rule and rules are obeyed only if they are supported by the ruled…or at least enough of the ruled to impose rules upon the rest. Power always follows

---

[23] "World" is used both here and in Colossians 2:8 as the expression of the kingdom of Satan on earth. You know this because it is contrasted with the "will of God."

persuasion. A ruler must convince others that his rules are right before they will follow him.

Persuasion is targeted at the intellect through reason and logic. But although all lawyers make a logical case does not necessarily make their case true. Reason may be used to sell a lie.

How can this be? How can worldviews that say opposing things all be logical? They can because they reason from certain assumptions or premises. And logic will follow whatever direction an assumption leads. Different assumptions lead to different conclusions.

Think about this.

How many times have you thought that a person is an idiot for what he believes? That is because his conclusions are at odds with your assumptions. But he does not believe your assumptions. He is as logical as you are.

Persuasion is the work of challenging assumptions and the resulting conclusions. Only an individual can decide to change their heart, but you can appeal to his conscience to make a correct judgement based on sound reasoning.

This is what the Apostle Paul did. He sought to persuade others of the truth about Jesus, as he did with King Agrippa.

> And Agrippa said to Paul, "In a short time would you **persuade** me to be a Christian?" And Paul said, "Whether short or long, I would to God that not only you but also all who hear me this day might become such as I am—except for these chains."
>
> Acts 26:28-29

You should read all of Acts chapter twenty-six for yourself. In it you will find a textbook case of how to persuade. Paul insists that he is "speaking true and rational words" that are verified by what is known. Furthermore, he communicates carefully, reasonably and respectfully to his audience. He understands their lawyers and makes the case why they should be replaced. All of these things are the elements of effective political persuasion.

Wait a minute! Paul is seeking a religious conversion not a change of mind on a political matter.

Conscience functions the same way regardless of the issue. Besides, I will argue that politics and religion are inherently inseparable. But you will have to wait until the next chapter to read about that.

For now remember this, every political argument is a logical appeal to conscience for justice.

CONSCIENCE AND JUSTICE

When Wrong Seems Wrong

I have described how conscience may render an incorrect verdict because of its lawyer. Someone may in good conscience believe or do something bad, just as Paul did when he was persecuting Christians. In this case, your goal is to persuade such a person that his reasoning is wrong and results in injustice. In other words, you are appealing to his conscience to make a right judgement.

But what if someone knows the arguments for justice, rejects them and pursues the unjust outcome anyway? The distinction is between being deceived by evil and actively pursuing it. This would have been the case if Paul had continued killing Christians after his Damascus road encounter with Jesus.

How do you respond to such a person?

Well…the most vivid answer is found in the Gospels.

The Gospels tell the story of the increasing rejection of Jesus by the Jewish leaders. In spite of the outward evidence of his miracles and the inward conviction of his words, they refused to repent and believe. They stubbornly clung to their lying lawyer. Eventually, out of the hardness of their hearts, they decided to kill Jesus.

How did Jesus respond? *Come on, fellas. Why get ugly? This makes me so uncomfortable! I'm fleeing to the wilderness where I can be meek and mild. Perhaps someone will paint that famous picture of me holding some cute little lamb.* No. Jesus rebuked the Jewish leaders in the strongest of terms.

> Woe to you, scribes and Pharisees, hypocrites! For you travel across sea and land to make a single proselyte, and when he becomes a proselyte, you make him twice as much a child of hell as yourselves.
>
> Matthew 23:15

Those are hard words! And he did not say them in private. Why not? Because the Jewish leaders were attacking Jesus and his message in public. They were trying to persuade the people to reject him. Jesus, in turn, discredited them by exposing the errors of their theology and morality. In front of everyone.

A pattern emerges in Jesus' response to others. He is gentle toward those who are open to his message. But he is increasingly stern toward those who reject it. Like this.

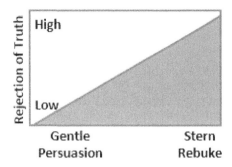

The horizontal axis describes the approach while the vertical axis describes the response. (I could also have labeled the vertical axis as "hardness of heart.") You should always operate as far to the left on this scale as possible. It is only in the face of opposition that you move to the right. In other words, you adjust how hard you push by how hard someone pushes back.

But what about the biblical command to live at peace with others?

Good question. Let's look at that.

> Repay no one evil for evil, but give thought to do what is honorable in the sight of all. If possible, so far as it depends on you, live peaceably with all. ...Do not be overcome by evil, but overcome evil with good.
> Romans 12:17-18, 21

Politics in the kingdom of the world is full of dirty tricks. It is not always clean. Nor fair. This should not surprise you, since it is a spiritual battleground between good and evil.

The passage above requires you to "live peaceably with all." You should not be a brawler, pugnacious nor any other word describing someone who is itching to pick a fight. No. You should—as a rule—be a gentle persuader.

However, there is a qualifier. "So far as it depends on you." This is significant. It could depend on you. You could be slandering a political opponent or distorting his position. But it does not always depend on you. Your opponent might attack you even when your behavior is exemplary. And when that happens, like Jesus, there are situations when you should punch back.

CONSCIENCE AND JUSTICE

The Further Adventures of Ebenezer Scrooge

I began this chapter with fiction, so it is only fitting to end with the same in order to wrap it up.

Let us examine...shall we say...Mr. Scrooge. Our Scrooge has a general interest in slavery and the slave trade, as do all British citizens, but he also has a financial interest. He personally profits from the trade.[24]

Scrooge faces two potential outcomes on the slavery issue.

First, the one we prefer. Scrooge's nephew, an abolitionist, visits. He pleads: "In the cause of all that is just, Uncle, you must oppose slavery. These people are human beings made in the image of God, as are you and I! Have mercy!"

Scrooge considers this, especially after being visited by the ghosts of slavery past, present and future. Scrooge: "I have been wrong on this matter! My conscience compels me to condemn slavery and this I do with my whole heart!" And so our hero buys the freedom of Bobeeb Cratchit and his crippled son Tiny Timbo. To top it off, he throws in a nice big goose for dinner.

Now for an alternate reality...well...not really a reality. Scrooge's conscience recognizes the justice of his nephew's case, but his heart is unwilling to change. Scrooge: "Blast my nephew and his mollycoddling! Blast those meddling busybody ghosts! And blast that slacker Cratchit and his wretched urchin Tiny Timbo! I will not be cheated out of my honest income! Bah humbug!"

Both scenarios begin with the disturbing of Scrooge's conscience. Who has upset it? The nephew. He has objected to injustice and Scrooge's role in it.

But why is Scrooge troubled about slavery? After all, his lawyer justifies it. And why does he give a hoot about what his nephew says? He could have said: "That is your personal religious belief, Nephew. Keep it to yourself and don't impose your scruples on me." And off he would go, calculating his profit or having a passing thought about his late partner Jacob Marley.

But this kind of detached indifference is not how Scrooge or anyone else reacts when the violation of a moral standard is exposed and their lawyer is revealed as a fraud. Why? Because conscience recognizes good and evil, especially when someone is rude enough to point it out.

Furthermore, a crisis arises. Conscience now forces an often difficult and painful choice between a softening of the heart or a hardening of it, between repentance toward God or rebellion against him, between getting

---

[24] I know that Dickens created Scrooge after the abolishment of the slave trade and slavery in Britain. So what? I can fictionalize fiction if I want to.

right or getting mad.

And if the choice is getting mad, that madness will often be directed at the one who pricks the conscience. That person in my little story was Scrooge's nephew. These days it should be you.

When you draw fire you may think that it is unfair. *Hey, don't shoot the messenger!* But while your opponent is ultimately shooting at God who made the standards, the bullet will often pass through you on the way there. It is a noble wound. And it is the cost of ruling the earth in righteousness.

Overcome evil with good in the political arena. And if you do, don't be surprised if it is not always possible to live peaceably with all.

* * *

Conscience is the moral reflection of God in man. Conscience interprets through a person's beliefs. These beliefs may be true or false. In politics, true beliefs lead to justice. False ones end in injustice. You have the responsibility, therefore, to defend what is true and just.

Every political argument is an appeal to conscience for justice. Everyone has a Jiminy Cricket.

24 Religion and Justice

I have a confession to make. I do not like the word "religion." In fact, I despise it.

I know that it is a perfectly good and useful word. Nevertheless, I get nauseous if someone describes me as "religious." I picture a religious person as someone in a clerical collar mumbling some nonsense about visualizing world peace. Or some snake-handling rube. Or some "fundamentalist" wearing an explosive vest.

Why all this negativity over a word that describes belief about God?

Well...the short answer is that there has been a successful campaign over the last three hundred years or so to characterize religion as being the refuge of ignorant, insecure, superstitious, unenlightened, weak-minded, anti-intellectual, repressive, oppressive, unstable, extremist and outright dangerous gap-toothed hillbillies and their kin, who are led by hypocritical shysters, militant clerics or other silver-tongued devils, and who want to drag everyone back into the horrors of the Dark Ages and torture dissenters on the rack, the wheel or, for good measure, the iron maiden, and force any fertile women to bear their children.

How did we get here? This is a long and detailed story that has a large cast of characters and has been described in many different ways. But since this is my book, I will tell the story as I see it. And since I like simplicity, I will shuck off the husk so that you can get right to the corn.

Consider my four-kingdom model once again.

THE KINGDOM OF THE WORLD

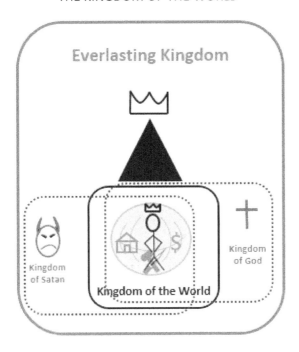

The Bible describes both physical and spiritual realities. Other religions construct different models, but most acknowledge some concept of God and of the spiritual. Of course they do. People created by God, in his image and for his glory inwardly know that there is something in addition to the kingdom of the world.

Along with this awareness, however, there is a strong desire in fallen humanity to usurp God, to rebel against him, to set themselves on his throne—an absurd *coup d'état* of sorts. This is the essence of the serpent's enticement to "be like God," which sounded like a pretty good idea to our first parents as they grasped at sin.

And so there is tension. On the one hand is man's innate knowledge that God exists, that he is the Creator, and that he rules over all with justice. On the other is man's determination to raise himself up to be like God, which always means lowering God to be like us.

A God I Can Live With

This raising of man and lowering of God is called idolatry. There are many versions of idolatry, but they all have one thing in common. Man creates God instead of the other way around. Man makes a God he prefers instead of acknowledging the real one.[25]

---

[25] See II Chronicles 32:19, Isaiah 2:8, Acts 7:41 and Revelation 9:20.

At its core, idolatry is about rulers, the ruled and rules. It is also about pride. When God makes man, God is the ruler and gets to make the rules. But if man makes God, man is entitled to do so. While this may seem bold and empowering in theory, it has one drawback in practice. It is all make-believe. A fantasy. Unreal. And it does not end well.

The crudest expression of idolatry is the physical idol. This is literally making the God you want…with your hands. These may be very massive or conveniently sized for home use. But for most people in Western nations, physical idols are only a matter of curiosity or tourism and not of worship.

In the West the idols are usually invisible not visible. This is closer to the truth in one sense. Jesus said to the woman at the well that "God is spirit, and those who worship him must worship in spirit and truth." He was, of course, referring to worshipping the God who exists rather than the ones that do not.

False Gods or idols may have a large following and may even have entire social structures built around them. But the real God does not reinvent himself when various religious interest groups try to define what he is and does. God is not swayed by public opinion. That is the thing about being God.

A growing expression of idolatry is "spirituality." No physical image is required. Nor is organized religion with all of its baggage, deserved or not. This person generates his own customized private beliefs. He picks and chooses whatever ones he desires, like filling his plate at a buffet. He forms a custom God for himself. Predictably, this God will reflect his creator. So I suppose that this God is not really invisible. This God always stares back from the mirror.

Spirituality religion thrives not only because it is compatible with our society's preoccupation with choice and consumption, but also because it is compatible with the idea that the individual reigns supreme over meaning and values.

This concept of the God-like individual creating his own religious reality is a popular belief nowadays. It is also the belief, not surprisingly, of those who claim that there is no God.

A God-less Religion

These are the same people who have made the term "religion" so loathsome. Who are they? They are the atheists. A "theist" is one who believes in God. Put an "a" in front of that and you have a person who does not.

But not really.

While monotheistic religions acknowledge a God above self, and polytheistic religions select a God preferred by self, and pantheistic religions make everything God including self, and spirituality religions fashion a God according to self, atheistic religion makes the pretense that they stand apart from all of this.

Isn't "atheistic religion" a contradiction, an oxymoron?

I think not. No one is more obsessed with God—the real one not the make-believes—than the atheist. Instead of making some ridiculous image, though, he decides to do away with God altogether.

Why? In order to take his place. While this is the goal of all idolatry, the atheist imagines that he can rule in God's place directly without any intermediaries or constraints. Like spirituality religion he thinks he can define reality as he sees fit. After all, man in his ignorance invented God in the first place, didn't he? And since man has evolved to a higher state, he can replace God altogether, can't he? *God is dead.* Or less deceitfully, *Man is God.*

This is religion pure and simple. It is also the ultimate in idolatry. It is the serpent's spiritual seduction: "You will be like God."

The atheist denies that his belief—or perhaps unbelief—is religious. But believing that man rules over God is as religious as believing that God rules over man. And the claim, "I don't believe in God," is absurd when the atheist is fixated on replacing someone he insists does not exist.

I am too polite to label such a person, but the Bible is not shy about it.

> The fool says in his heart, "There is no God."
> Psalm 14:1

For one who makes such a poor life choice, his next step is to recruit others to join him. There is safety in numbers, isn't there? If not safety, at least some measure of camaraderie. So the atheist tries to convince his fellow image bearers of God of something they know is not true—that there is no spiritual aspect of life, that there is nothing more than matter. Anything that is not physical cannot exist in the atheist's construct. There is no creator of creation. There is no designer of design. There is only chance plus time. Matter in movement. Math.

In other words, the atheist concocts a one-kingdom view of reality. And no one is more aggressive in evangelizing than the atheist.

The Problem of Evil

He does this in many ways. I will mention only a few.

The atheist has made a philosophical case against God based on the existence of evil. His argument is basically that a good God would not allow evil and since there is evil, there is no God. But this argument only works within a certain context—a context that begins and ends with the here and now. Since there is nothing other than the physical world and since there is injustice in this world, there is no just God. In other words, the atheist imagines a world without God and then uses this God-less world to disprove God.

If atheists were better theologians, they would have pondered the biblical four-kingdom view of reality a little more thoroughly. And if they were wiser, they would have hesitated to condemn the purposes and workings of God based on their limited perspective of what he should be doing. But the biggest weakness of their argument becomes apparent if you flip it over. On the other side of if-there-is-evil-there-can-be-no-God is if-there-is-no-God-there-can-be-no-evil.

News Flash: Evil is not physical. It is moral. Which is spiritual. Everything physical—matter—is neither good nor evil. It is amoral. It is neutral. When the atheist cites evil, he backhandedly acknowledges that there is more than the physical world. There are spiritual realities…which contradict his basic assumption about God.

Besides, the argument from evil often flows from reasons that are more personal than philosophical anyway. *I am angry at God for the injustices I have experienced or that I see around me…so I will eliminate him.* Once again, the atheist's problem with admitting this is, of course, that he must concede God before liquidating him.

THE KINGDOM OF THE WORLD

The Cloak of Science

Whether the argument from evil serves as expression of anger against God or an amusing parlor game for half-insane philosophers and the wide-eyed college freshmen who consume them, it has not been particularly effective in capturing the popular imagination. Atheists need something that is less abstract and that avoids all of the silly questions about the meaning and purpose of life.

Which brings us to science.

Science is a systematic approach to discovering truths about physical properties. It involves observation and experimentation, known as the "scientific method." Science grew and flourished in a Western culture that generally accepted that God is distinct from his creation. Matter is neither God nor an illusion. Science is a means of fulfilling the Dominion Mandate to rule the earth. In this context, science is viewed as discovering God's design. Science, as a result, is beneficial—not only by increasing knowledge but by providing many useful applications.

The atheists are no dummies. They recognize an opportunity when they see one. Science had cred. They needed this credibility to sell their belief in a God-less world. And so began the most successful bait-and-switch scheme in human history. The bait is science. The switch is atheism.

The trick was to make their atheistic beliefs indistinguishable from empirical science. Here are some examples of how this works.

> Just as scientists measure the exact rate of an apple falling to the ground, so they calculate how and when nothing created itself into the universe.
>
> Just as scientists observe that finches adapt to different environments, so they know that—given enough time—amoeba evolve into software engineers.
>
> Just as scientists describe the social interaction in prairie dog colonies, so they can reduce all human behavior to survival and sex instincts.

Note that the "just as" phrase is actual science. Such observations can be repeated or falsified through experimentation. The "so they" phrase cannot be. These are just assertions extrapolated from atheistic assumptions disguised as science. The first example supports a God-less explanation for existence. The second supports a God-less explanation for humanity. And the third supports a God-less explanation for morality.

You seldom hear any evidence that challenges assumptions about a completely naturalistic world. This is not because there is no evidence that points in another direction. It is because these assumptions are rarely questioned. In the instances when you hear evidence to the contrary, it is usually when someone is promoting an alternate or revised atheistic theory in order to address evidence that can no longer be ignored. *We were wrong about this detail, but now we really know how it happened.*

The significance of such inconsistences and changes are often missed. Or they are simply ignored. These are mere technical details that most people are unconcerned with. After all, the "scientists" know what they are talking about, don't they?

There is another reason—a better one—why the atheist's narrative is so widely accepted. The material world *appears* to be moving along under its own momentum apart from the working of God. This is how life is experienced. We do not see the hand of God. It is invisible.

Hold on! First you said that people have an awareness of God, which is why they are idolaters, and now you say that most of them are atheists. You can't have it both ways.

I'm glad that you are still paying attention. It shows a mental toughness. But you must have dozed off a bit because I did not say that most people are atheists. Most are only pressured to act like them in public.

I can see that you are going to struggle with this. So before I continue, why don't you grab a cup of coffee. This is going to require all of your powers.

* * *

Good to go?
Just get on with it!

The Myth of Non-Moral Morality

I am amused whenever an atheist complains that so many people still cling to religion. The atheist thinks that his logic has been so compelling and his science so irrefutable that no rational person would retain religious superstitions. But that is not what is funny.

What is funny is that even though his ideas dominate public life he is still such a whiner. After all, it is the atheist's perspective that is taught and reinforced throughout our cultural institutions.

This atheistic environment has been so prevalent for so long that you hardly think about it anymore. You just accept it. The creating and sustaining God of the universe is excluded from the classroom, the boardroom, the breakroom, the courtroom and the news room. Religious beliefs must be confined safely within the private world of thoughts and feelings. They must not intrude on the "real" world.

This creates a problem.

Religious beliefs are the source of both private and public morality. Consider this one from the Ten Commandments: "You shall not murder." There is a personal application. *I shall not murder.* And a political application. *Government shall prevent murder when possible or punish the murderer.*

If the atheist was consistent, he would say that your belief that God commands you not to murder is fine for your personal behavior. But you cannot force others to conform to your belief. How then does the atheist justify forcing everyone to conform to his belief against murder?

I will let the atheist speak for himself. But first the biblical case.

> God has made man in his image and this image distinguishes man from all the rest of creation, giving him not just unique value but also great responsibility. This responsibility includes ruling the earth with justice, in submission to God and in respect for fellow man. Murder is an attack on the image of God in man and a corruption of the rule of man. While God will execute the ultimate judgement for this transgression, government is required to punish the murderer now.

The biblical case is based upon spiritual assumptions. I count at least seven of them here. The atheist says that these spiritual assumptions cannot be used to justify rules that govern social behavior. But his beliefs can, of course. Here now is the atheist. He must make a case solely upon the basis of matter in motion. Good luck.

> Scientists have studied prairie dogs and have learned that they organize socially for mutual protection and propagation. From this we can derive that humans should cooperate together for the overall benefit of the species. As murder tends to disrupt cooperation, it should be discouraged by the social order.

You may have noticed that the atheist's case against murder is rather flimsy. The more you think about it, the weaker it gets. Besides, if he really wanted to follow the logic of his assumptions, his morality would be along the lines of "survival of the fittest." Go ahead and knock off the weak so that the strong may thrive. But this approach has already been tried in history and its results have been so horrifying that most people disavow the concept. Even the atheists. For the moment.

This leaves political debate a bit convoluted. A spiritual foundation for justice must not be spoken because it is "religious." Morality identified as having its basis in the Bible is ridiculed in public discourse. But rodent-based ethics or other naturalistic explanations for morality that are culturally sanctioned are unconvincing at best.

This also explains why moral norms are so fluid when atheism shapes culture. Without a permanent foundation for justice, what was considered to be immoral yesterday becomes a human right today. And what is accepted as good today will be despised as evil tomorrow. Ethics that are not grounded in spiritual and universal truths are easily maneuvered to justify any behavior that becomes fashionable at the moment.

All of this places the dominant atheistic culture in conflict with biblical morality.

Public and Private Morality

Another lie is that public and private morality are separable. They are not. One influences the other. Like this.

Behavior is influenced internally by the judgement of conscience and externally by government, which has the power to impose its rules by force. There are additional influences on behavior, especially the institutions of family and church. The heart takes all of these under consideration when determining to do good or evil.

This picture also shows that political involvement flows from beliefs, since beliefs form the understanding of justice. But it is also true that government exerts pressure to conform beliefs to its rules. If the government says something is right or wrong, it is...isn't it? This is positive pressure when the rules are just. But when the rules are unjust, you are forced to choose between following conscience to do what is good and suffer the consequences or to disobey conscience in order to escape unjust punishment. A tough choice.

I think the atheist would agree with my little illustration. For him. Not for you. He thinks that his beliefs should shape politics and that his politics should shape your beliefs. But yours should not. Why? Because your beliefs are "religious" and his, supposedly, are not.

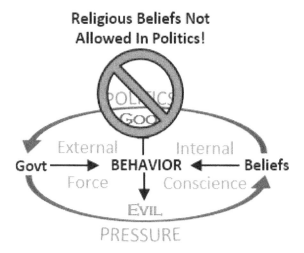

This is a brilliant play. The easiest way to defeat your opponent is to disqualify him from the contest.

Does this surprise you? It should not. Atheism is a rival belief system. A competitor of Christianity. (I speak of the Western atheist. I know little of the other species.)

The atheist's beliefs are a reaction against the biblically-influenced culture out of which he sprang. He is not threatened by religious teaching that promotes withdrawal and disassociation from the kingdom of the world. Those people are harmless and easily subjected. And strangely enough, he often ignores religions, such as Islam, which pose a very real physical and political danger to him.

Perhaps you think that I am overreacting or excessively sensitive or insecure. That may be, but I am still right about the atheist's determination to silence beliefs he opposes. The proof is in four common sayings.

Half Truths and Whole Lies

There is some truth in the first three of the sayings. About half. In each case the true half disguises the lies. The true half is intended to trick conscience into accepting the whole bundle, which is how the devil likes to package his politics. The fourth saying is so embarrassing that it should make even the Great Deceiver blush.

Here is the first one.

RELIGION AND JUSTICE

The Separation of Church and State.

The true half of this one is that religion should be institutionally distinct from government. The false half is that religion should be influentially excluded from politics.

The lie is that if a church addresses political issues—critiquing rulers and rules—then it is usurping the state. But moral teaching is not the same thing as governmental authority. Wielding the Bible is not wielding the sword. Persuading is not punishing.

As I said earlier in this book, the consistent and repeated instruction in the New Testament is to support the dominion institutions not supplant them.

For example, when a church instructs the family on morality—husbands love your wives, wives submit to your husbands, children obey your parents—is the church commandeering the authority that belongs within family relationships? No, it is not. A church does not assume the roles and responsibilities of husband, wife, parent and child. The family is accountable under God to obey these commands. But the church is responsible to teach them.

It is the same when a church exhorts it members to faithfully fulfill their government responsibilities. When church members do politics, they are not overthrowing the government and establishing a theocracy. They are exercising their role as citizens. They may be informed by a church, but everyone is informed by the various organizations and influences that share their beliefs.

I will only mention in passing that throughout history civil power has jumped around among and between the dominion institutions. Sometimes governing power goes from the smaller unit to the larger unit—from family to clan to tribe to king to emperor. But if a larger unit breaks down, a smaller unit may regain control in the ensuing chaos.

This is to say that the contest over government authority is ongoing and continuously changing. A church should never compete in this game.

Unfortunately, some have. Churches have taken hold of the sword. And they have done so to use civil penalties, including death, to impose the faith. The problem here, of course, is that faith cannot be imposed. It must be believed. That is true of all beliefs, even atheistic ones. Government may force outward conformance. But it can never mandate true belief. Conscience must be persuaded.

The Two Swords theology of the Roman Catholic Church that I described in Chapter 11 is an example of attempting to impose belief through government force. Civil rulers were fragmented and relatively weak after the collapse of the Roman Empire. In comparison the Roman Catholic Church was unified and relatively strong. This enabled the pope to sometimes control the kings. While the kings did not always submit and sometimes sent the pope scurrying, on the whole, church rulers exercised ruling power over government rulers.

But this is not the ruling power of churches sanctioned in the New Testament. How does a church respond to someone who refuses to obey church rulers and rules? By fines, imprisonment or execution? No. Significantly, it is by kicking the rebellious person out of the church. This is called "church discipline" or "shunning" or "excommunication." *Since you refuse to obey our rulers and rules, you are no longer subject to them.* Exclusion not physical force.

The atheist makes a fair point when he condemns a church for wielding the sword. But he overdoes it. Christian history consists of more than the Inquisition and the Salem witch trials...although you may not realize this from the schooling you received.

More significantly, the atheist's intense desire to discredit Christianity blinds him to his own faults. Government injustice committed by churches pales in comparison to the oppression achieved by the atheist. He should pay attention to the log in his own eye, as Jesus said.

Consider the totalitarian governments of recent history, beginning with the French Revolution. These states attempted to impose not just obedience necessary for civil order but conformity of thought and belief to the policies of the state. As Benito Mussolini said: "Everything within the state, nothing outside the state, nothing against the state." Such elegance describes totalitarian government of every flavor.

What is the common denominator among these governments? Atheism. They may be officially atheistic states, like communism, or just atheistic in thought and practice, like fascism, but they all have the same creed. *What is the chief end of man? To serve the state and worship its rulers.* The state—the unified man—becomes God. The state is the focus of every hope, the fulfiller of every need, the purpose of life.

Until they collapse, that is.

I am not saying that the common go-with-the-cultural-flow atheist or even every ideological true-believer atheist is a Jacobin or fascist or communist.[26] After all, even the atheist has a conscience and eventually recognizes injustice. *Hmmm...we must not be doing this right.* But I am saying

---

[26] There is, of course, no universal atheist. While atheists agree on their denial of God, they disagree on many other things...just like normal people. Take government. Not all atheists are totalitarians. Many are attracted by the glow of the sovereign state but some fly toward sovereign individualism in opposition to the state. But my interest is the impact of atheistic culture on politics. And because of this, my atheist will move with the herd and not stray away with the loners.

that the atheist—lacking an institutional home for his beliefs—has put all his energy into appropriating government for this purpose.

In order to be fair, I must again allow the atheist to speak for himself, lest you think that I am misrepresenting him.

> Ever hear of the Inquisition or the Salem witch trials? You religious people are a threat to the common good and individual freedom. Better to have rational individuals like myself in charge than oppressors like you. You may teach whatever beliefs you want in private but keep them out of the public. My beliefs dominate there. I own the social institutions. So while you are busy talking in your little church, I am pulling the levels of real power. In my direction. Too bad for you. Your time was the Dark Ages. Mine is now.

Well…the atheist is right about a few things here. Ruling power belongs to whoever wins it through the political process…and he has been on a winning streak lately. And whoever rules over government uses it to form governing rules in accordance with his beliefs. To the victor belong the spoils, it is said.

This has always been true, but it takes on greater significance with bigger government. Why? Because when government rules reach into every area of life, everything becomes political because politics determines those rules.

Politics would be less incendiary today if there were less at stake. Would everyone get so worked up if the only political issues were about who should manage the sewer plant, the correct number of tanks for the army, and debates about a law against sleeping on the park bench? I think not.

But government has expanded far beyond the functions of infrastructure, defense and crime. It now provides for private welfare in addition to public welfare. And most importantly, government is the primary provider and controller of what is taught in school. Why is this significant? Because what is taught in school is somebody's beliefs.

Guess whose.

It is not the creation story you believe. It is not that man is made in the image of God yet fallen. It is not biblical morality. It is the atheist's version of all of these.

Which brings me to the second common saying, which is closely related to the first.

Religion and politics don't mix.

What is true about this second saying is the same thing that was true in the first one. Church and state should be institutionally distinct. But the lie is subtly different.

The first lie was that because a church is a "religious" institution it should not be permitted to influence politics by instructing its members. The second lie is not directed at the role of the church but on the Christian himself. A person's religious beliefs should not be permitted to influence his politics.

If the atheist said this outright, his case would not be very convincing. Why should his beliefs be allowed to compete in public matters and other beliefs disqualified? So the atheist redefines the terms of the debate, always a clever and effective technique.

His beliefs, you see, are not beliefs.

They are facts.

Facts supported by science…as he defines science.

Facts that are arrived at solely through reason.

And reason is the enemy of religion, as everyone knows. Because religion is irrational, emotional, hillbillyish, dangerous, etc., etc., etc.

Such a brilliant argument. But it has one weakness. Everyone is reasonable. The atheist misses this obvious point because religious conclusions conflict with his assumptions.

I have a pet peeve along this line. It is the expression "a senseless act of violence." No act of violence is senseless. It makes perfect sense to the person deliberately doing it. Otherwise he would not be doing it. But it doesn't make sense—it isn't rational—to the person who has different beliefs and, therefore, would never do such a thing and cannot imagine why anyone would.

This is a lack of understanding not a lack of logic.

But the atheist assumes that beliefs other than his own are crazy. And he probably believes that his beliefs are actually empirical facts. After all, he has been so thoroughly and uniformly indoctrinated from an atheistic perspective that he cannot see beyond the tip of his own nose.

It is just as reasonable to believe that God created man, that man rebelled against God resulting in death, that Jesus died in order to reconcile man to God, that you must humble yourself before God and choose to believe these things, and that they are proven true by the resurrection of Jesus from the dead, as it is to believe that there is no God, that the marvelous complexity and interdependence of what exists is nothing other than matter in motion, which somehow created itself, and that the purpose to life is to advance mankind in a purposeless universe.

The atheist repurposing his beliefs as reason is as misleading as cloaking them in science.

Religion and politics always mix.

Which brings us to the third common saying.

RELIGION AND JUSTICE

You can't legislate morality.

This one requires less explanation.

The lie first. The lie is that public governance has nothing to do with moral standards. Morality, it is said, is religious and religion must not be imposed on the public through government rules.

There is one problem here. Do you see it? It is that all rules express what a society defines as just or unjust. That is, they define what is right or wrong and good or evil…which is the definition of morality.

News Flash: All rules are inherently moral.

Legislation is morality. Whose morality? Whoever wins the political contest.

In order to wring some truth out of "you can't legislate morality," you must change its meaning to "you can't force everyone to obey legislation." Of course not! There are rules against murder but people still commit murder. But should rules be eliminated because some people disobey them? That is absurd.

Rules always disincentivize or incentivize behavior. I will illustrate this with something less serious than murder. If you disincentivize the eating of tofu through execution or prison time, you will get less tofu eating in a society. The personal cost is high. Plus, you will send the moral message that tofu consumption is evil. But if you incentivize tofu eating through tax breaks, a society will eat more of it. The personal benefit is high. Plus, you will send the moral message that tofu is virtuous.

So the rules really do influence behavior. They just do not determine all behavior. Some people will still break the rules.

In the end, "you can't legislate morality" is just another political ploy by those trying to silence the influence of morality they disagree with in order to impose their own morality.

Unfortunately there is a "spiritual" version of this saying. And perhaps you believe it. *You can't change hearts through legislation.* This is obviously true, but…so what?

Rules are primarily directed at outward behavior not heart change. The government cannot control what you believe, think or desire. All the dominion institutions—government, family and employment—can only define rules that affect your outward behavior. Should rules be considered useless because they are not followed wholeheartedly? See how that works out with your two-year old or teenager.

Outward rules have never shaped the heart. There is no greater demonstration of this than the Old Testament. Moses' law defined outward conformance but could not create an inward love for God. A heart that loves God and, therefore, obeys him is the work of God's grace—a new heart, a heart of flesh—not the result of man's works. Love for God must proceed from the inside out not the outside in.

One more half-truth. And you may own this one too. Perhaps you have said, *There is no sense in trying to change laws unless hearts are changed first. Converted hearts will eventually result in better laws.* This is true on an individual level. A person that believes the gospel will be transformed by the grace of God, including his political perspective.

But the rules themselves are always just or unjust. Now. Just rules honor God and respect your neighbor. Now. Unjust rules dishonor God and harm your neighbor. Now. You have a social responsibility to rule justly, as much as you are able. Now.

I will not allow my faith to influence my politics.

This last saying is one that you hear from professional politicians. It is stated in many different ways but the gist is that the politician will not impose his religion—his beliefs—on others.

Which is so transparently disingenuous.

Politicians politic for the same reason writers write and preachers preach and teachers teach and orators orate and agitators agitate and spinners spin and late-night comedians mock. To promote their beliefs.

I am not criticizing this. If you believe something is right, you naturally want others to believe it too. And you should work to have your beliefs reflected in society's rules.

So when a politician uses this line he is almost always trying to cover up his deceit. Rather than analyzing the lie, I will just restate it for you in honest language.

> I always tailor my words to the audience so that they will think that we believe the same things. I'll throw out a few of their catch phrases and key words...like whistling for a dog. Religious people are always so grateful for the attention. But when I talk to those I truly agree with, I assure them that I never really meant any of that stuff. So I use code that they understand: *Don't worry. After the useful idiots help elect me, I will carry out my—and your—real agenda.*

Less cynically, there is another possible meaning. The politician may be saying that if he obtains a ruling position he will enforce the rules—even rules that he disagrees with. This is honorable. This is called "the rule of law." The alternative is either corruption or chaos. Lawlessness. He should, of course, work within the rules to change the rules to conform to his beliefs. But if that is his intention, he should say so plainly. And leave the weasel words to the weasels.

*   *   *

This has been a long and somewhat complex chapter. Unavoidably so, given that so many lies are woven throughout the dominant atheistic culture. *Religion is discredited by science. Religion is opposed to reason. And religion should be excluded from politics.* But belief about God—even the belief that he does not exist—is always the primary shaper of a society's morality. That is, religion is inseparable from politics…as well as from everything else.

But the atheist insists that it has no public place in his one-kingdom view of reality.

25 Love and Justice

One common religious teaching is universally recognized as essential for good politics.

Jesus stated it in two slightly different ways. One wording is known as the Second Greatest Commandment. "Love your neighbor as yourself."[27] The other is known as the Golden Rule. "So whatever you wish that others would do to you, do also to them."[28] Similar phrasings are found throughout the world's religions.

Some say that this is the one indispensable feature of all religion and that any additional beliefs are unnecessary, divisive and should be discarded, which is a good summary of theological liberalism. But stripping religion of everything but the Second Greatest Commandment/Golden Rule is like taking a train off of its track. It is not coming from or going anywhere. The reasons for the command have been removed. All that is left is: "Be nice…just because."

The biblical reason for the Second Greatest Commandment is the First Greatest Commandment. "And you shall love the Lord your God with all your heart and with all your soul and with all your mind and with all your strength."[29] Love for God and love for neighbor are inseparable. The second flows out of the first. Love for God is displayed in loving those who are made in his image. You cannot love God and hate your neighbor.

The second commandment is the guiding principle that covers all human interaction. It applies to rulers and the ruled alike. It is the foundation for the more specific commands regarding social relationships, such as: honor and obey those in authority; don't lie, cheat or steal; care for

---

[27] See Matthew 22:39.
[28] See Matthew 7:12.
[29] See Mark 12:30.

the weak and protect the defenseless; etc.

Furthermore, the larger biblical narrative provides an entire framework for loving God and neighbor—creation, the Dominion Mandate, man's fall, salvation in Jesus, the final judgement, the new heavens and earth. And all of this is occurring under the sovereign rule of a just God.

God-less Love

I am sure that other religions have some sort of rationale behind their own love-your-neighbor commands. And I am sure that these reasons share some similarities with the biblical command, just as counterfeit bills bear resemblance to real ones. But how does the atheist, who denies his responsibility under God, explain why he should love his neighbor? Well…his official response is that this urge is encoded in human DNA to ensure the survival of the species…very similar to the cooperation observed in prairie dog colonies. Human moral behavior is not moral at all, you see. It is just another version of animal instincts.

Despite all of their atheistic schooling, however, humans instinctively—if I may use the term—understand that a man is not a pig with thumbs. He is created in the image of God and all that is good or evil in the world is evidence of his spiritual struggle over doing one or the other. He knows that treating other people justly is right and treating them unjustly is wrong.

The atheist's attempts to persuade humans to act like non-humans in order to achieve good social order has fallen on deaf ears. Whenever humans associate other humans with non-humans, it is to dehumanize the humans not to inspire them. And the purpose of dehumanizing them is to quiet conscience's protests about the injustice being committed upon them. *Enslave the monkeys! Kill the cockroaches! Eliminate the vermin!*

Lies about the nature of man will sooner or later inspire acts of injustice.

And speaking of lies, another pack of whoppers turns the Second Greatest Commandment/Golden Rule upside down and inside out. How? By redefining the meaning of words.

Who Is My Neighbor?

The simplest way to avoid loving your neighbor is to deny that he is your neighbor. *I don't have to treat him as I want to be treated.* Why not? *Because he is from a different neighborhood.*

If you are an observer of culture you may think that politics are increasingly polarized, vicious and tribalized. This is true, of course…except for the "increasingly" part.

Throughout history people have considered others outside their own group as non-neighbors. They may be viewed as competitors, at best, or threats that must be eliminated, at worst. These "others" are distinguished from neighbors by their differences—in language, customs, class, religion or even such superficial characteristics as skin color.

There is no need—it is assumed—to love those "others." They are not neighbors. And since they are not, they may be treated badly.

You should be able to see the political application here. You do not have to search long nor hard to find abuses of one group against another…or when your own group has been mistreated. These injustices are often exploited for political purposes. *They have oppressed us and now it is our turn to oppress them. So we are justified in being unjust. It's payback time!* But this grievance-retribution cycle only perpetuates the hatred. Like a blood feud.

Jesus radically challenged this ethic. He answered the question of "Who is my Neighbor?" in the parable of the good Samaritan.

A lawyer asked Jesus what he must do to inherit eternal life. Jesus, in turn, asked him what Moses' law teaches. The lawyer answered correctly that the law requires obedience to the two great commandments. Love God. Love your neighbor. The lawyer should have sat down at this point. But, as lawyers tend to do, he kept talking. "And who is my neighbor?"

And now the parable. A man—a Jew—was traveling when thieves attacked. They robbed, stripped and left him half dead. A priest and then a Levite passed by the man, moving to the other side of the road so as to not get too close to him—a poor showing by these religious fellows. Then a third man comes along. A Samaritan.

A word about Samaritans. The Jews did not think Samaritans as neighbors. Ethnic differences? Check. Religious differences? Check. They had a long history of hostility. Bad blood. Really bad. But in Jesus' parable it is the Samaritan who stops, binds the man's wounds, takes him to an inn, and pays for his care.

If I had written this parable, I would have had the Samaritan robbed and left half alive. I think this would have played better with the Jewish audience. A Jew would have been the hero in my version. The humble and righteous Jewish man demonstrates his good character by caring for the despicable, filthy, heretical Samaritan. But Jesus had it the other way around. The Samaritan served the Jew.

Who proved himself to be the neighbor? The priest? No. The Levite? No. It was the Samaritan.

The point, which even the lawyer got, is that everyone is your neighbor. EVERYONE.

But the parable is not about politics, which is what you are supposed to be writing about. Government is not involved. This is a case of private charity. Individual to individual.

Very impressive. You are learning. I can see that my work here is almost done.

Parables make a point. The point here is that everyone is your neighbor and, therefore, you are required to love them. This is disciplined biblical interpretation.

But having been disciplined, I will now wander into some unwarranted speculation. Why didn't the priest and Levite help the Jewish man? They had social responsibilities to their people. Perhaps they thought something like this. *What are we paying such outrageous taxes to the Romans for? Let the state care for him.*

And notice what the Samaritan did not do. He did not track down the thieves and punish their crime. He did not become a vigilante, usurping the role and responsibility of government rulers.

These questions really have nothing to do with the parable, but they do raise the issue of government and love. How do rulers love their neighbors when ruling? And what does that look like? Or to put it another way, is justice compatible with love?

I'll get to that shortly, but first let's examine the other big word in the command.

What is Love?

The Bible describes different types of love. There is romantic love. There is brotherly love. And concerning our topic, there is the love that treats others as you would like to be treated, that does what is best for them, that puts their interests above your own. This last definition of love is the one that applies to politics.

> Love does no wrong to a neighbor; therefore love is the fulfilling of the law.
>
> Romans 13:10

> Let each of us please his neighbor for his good, to build him up.
>
> Romans 15:2

There are negative and positive tests here. "No wrong." "For his good." If an action fulfills these criteria, you are truly loving your neighbor.

But the common understanding of love nowadays is much different. It focuses solely on the "please his neighbor" part without the moral qualifiers. Love has come to mean that you must accept whatever one believes and support however he behaves. In other words, you must make him happy.

This is not love.

When a person believes a lie it is not love to tell him that it is "true for him." It is love to expose the lie so that he will not be deceived by it. When a person acts in a way that that harms himself or others, it is not love to celebrate his expression of "self-fulfillment." It is love to warn him of his self-destructive and harmful behavior.

But nowadays, if you disapprove of or refuse to participate in another's sinful actions, you are labeled a "hater." You are the threat to society. Your opinion is an act of violence against others. You are the one that must be silenced and restrained by the rules.

Love is condemned as hate. Hate is disguised as love. The world is upside down, inside out. And the devil laughs.

Love Your Neighborhood

If loving your neighbor is hard, loving your neighborhood is harder. That is, your personal response to another individual is easier to figure out than your political role that affects the whole of society.

Why is that?

To begin with, there is widespread belief that punishment is unloving. Punishment is opposed to love. After all, isn't "government a necessary evil?" If government is evil, then the actions of government are evil. Justice is evil. But necessary.

This causes such confusion.

Why do so many people believe such a lie? Because it is repeated so constantly and cleverly.

<u>Warning</u>: What I am about to say may be deeply offensive to you…if you cherish Victor Hugo's beloved novel *Les Misérables* (and the popular musical version). The two main characters in *Les Misérables* are in conflict throughout the story. Jean Valjean represents love of neighbor. Inspector Javert represents the state. Valjean is grace. Javert is law. Valjean good. Javert bad.

In the interest of conciseness, I will not summarize the whole story but will skip to the end, which is my way of saying "spoiler alert." Valjean having received grace gives grace. He loves his neighbor. He even extends it to his great enemy and tormentor Javert. But Javert—the man of law and justice—is unable to accept it…and so he kills himself.

In case you have still missed it, the point is that love and justice are at odds.

But they are not.

What makes this difficult to discern in *Les Misérables* and in life in general is that the law is not always just. The rules are not always fair. Javert was enforcing some unjust and unfair rules. And when this is the case, law becomes a means of oppression. This is not love of neighbor.

True justice always improves a neighborhood. Injustice degrades it.

More injustice results in more corruption, crime, destitution and despair. If you love your neighbor, you must work to improve the neighborhood not degrade it.

A Case Study

Let's see how this plays out in real life...well...in my active imagination anyway. Consider a governor. I'll name him Governor Luvall. The governor issues a moratorium on executions. No murderer will be put to death in his state. Being a politician, he holds a press conference to explain his decision.

I will give his reasons and then critique them. Reason One: *Sometimes there are mistakes.* That is true, of course. The error may be unintentional or malicious. But this rationale could be used to eliminate all penalties of all crimes. It is better to work to ensure justice than to eliminate it. Reason Two: *Some people groups are disproportionally impacted by capital punishment.* This is seeking justice through statistics, which is unjust. God judges the individual for what he does, not what others have or have not done. Justice requires treating a person as a moral being responsible for his actions. Reason Three: *It is barbaric. It is lowering the society to the brutality of the murderer.* But punishment for a crime is not the same thing as committing the crime. And it is not cruel to administer a just punishment.

The fourth, and last, reason is the one I want to focus on. *I do not have the right to take another human life.* Here the governor is attempting to erase the distinction between his private actions and his official duties. Luvall—the individual—has no right to kill the murderer. If he were to burst into the murderer's cell, yell "Die scumbag!" and empty his revolver into the criminal, Luvall would be a murderer too. Execution must be by the state in accordance with the rules of the state. If Luvall "took the law into his own hands," as the saying goes, he would deserve the same fate as the murderer.

But when Luvall is acting in his official role as governor, he is exercising the authority given to him by God to maintain necessary order in society. If the governor does not fulfill his duty, he should be removed from office. Which raises another point.

The governor's action may, of course, be motivated by something else. Not justice but politics. Not love but power. Governors and other high officials are not usually dummies. They are pretty good at taking the pulse of the people who elect them. If the people clamor for injustice, the governor gives them what they want so that they will give him what he wants. *Quid pro quo.* Both sides of the ruler-ruled dynamic bear responsibility.

Whatever Luvall's reasons, his refusal to exercise his office justly is not love. And since he is under God, he will give account for his actions to God.

Tough Love

So are you saying that when a governor orders an execution he is loving his neighbor? That is hard to swallow. The neighborhood may be better but that neighbor dies. How can that be love?

Well…it sure isn't the happiness type of love. Few people bubble over with delight when feeling the sword of justice. But it is what is best for them.

Justice teaches the hard lesson that there is right and wrong and that there is a price to pay for doing evil. There is a price to pay now in the kingdom of the world before man. And as the temporal reflects the eternal, there is an ultimate price to pay before God.

Justice is painful medicine but it is medicine that will heal when accepted.

> Some sat in darkness and in the shadow of death,
> prisoners in affliction and in irons,
> for they had rebelled against the words of God,
> and spurned the counsel of the Most High.
> So he bowed their hearts down with hard labor;
> they fell down, with none to help.
>
> Then they cried to the LORD in their trouble,
> and he delivered them from their distress.
> He brought them out of darkness and the shadow of death, and burst their bonds apart.
>
> Let them thank the LORD for his steadfast love,
> for his wondrous works to the children of man!
>
> Psalms 107:10-15

The psalmist draws back the curtain to reveal the spiritual realities in play. The prisoners were in prison because they had broken the rules of the kingdom of the world. But their rebellion was ultimately against God. And their human punishment was from God.

What was the prisoners' response? "They cried out to the Lord." In other words, they repented. They turned away from their sin and turned toward God. How do we know that? Because of God's response. Mercy. Which is always his response when anyone humbles himself. And the imagery here indicates that they received more than a get-out-of-jail card. Eternal destinies are at stake.

The final verse I cited is the most surprising. It speaks of God's "steadfast love" and "wondrous works." For prison and hard labor? Yes…and the good that resulted from these. If God's justice is motivated by love, its exercise on earth should be also.

This is not to say that justice always results in repentance. It often does not. A person may harden his heart and become more rebellious and angry at God. A fool rejects what God provides for his benefit.

If You Love Me…

Nothing is more political than sex these days. I don't mean sex sex but the social rules regarding child bearing, relationships, roles and marriage. Even biology is being denied as people seek to create their own reality for these matters. This is just one more expression of the idolatry of self.

> If you loved me, you would support me in being who I want to be and in doing what I want to do. But since you hate me, you condemn me. I now have the freedom in this country to live the way I want…as long as it doesn't hurt anyone else. The days when you could tyrannize me are over. Your violence must be stopped. The oppressor must be oppressed. Society is now enlightened and free.

Hey! You promised no controversial issues.

I speak only in generalities. And I only bring this up because nowhere does make-me-happy love contrast more with love-your-neighbor love.

Before I address what love requires, think about what is underneath such sexual activism. It is public approval for behavior that was once disapproved by the culture and disincentivized by the rules. But now it is behavior that is largely approved by the culture and incentivized by the rules. So why is it even an issue any longer if some people—such as you, I hope—still uphold biblical morality?

Conscience.

Despite the great surrounding web of lies, the sexual activist's conscience still troubles him…especially when you say something that resonates with his conscience, which is what truth does. It reawakens conscience's protest and warning, which is upsetting. *I just want to be happy!*

Unfortunately, the activist does not look inward. He looks outward. He thinks that you are the problem. He thinks that if he can silence you, he can silence his conscience. So he puts his energy into politics. Rules are needed to keep you quiet. And if he has enough political success, he will get those rules.

Did you catch that? The activist claims that it is unjust for society to "legislate morality." That is, it is wrong to make rules prohibiting the sexual practices he prefers. So…he wants to make new rules prohibiting your disapproval of his sexual practices.

News Flash: All societies make rules about sexual behavior…as this proves. Prohibited behavior is criminalized. Beneficial behavior—traditionally concerning marriage and children—is incentivized. Human rules do not make something good or evil, of course, but they promote one or the other. In any case, when what is considered to be right or wrong in society is in transition, the contest over the rules that define that these things become political battles.

The irony for the sexual activist is that if he gets the rules he wants, he will make his situation worse not better. Despite what the culture tells him, his immoral behavior will not deliver what it promises. Instead of the imagined happiness he seeks, it will sooner or later lead to disappointment, regret and, perhaps, despair. Sin may taste sweet at first, but it always turns bitter in the end.

And it is not only bad for your neighbor but also for the entire neighborhood. The nobody-is-harmed-by-it argument is a lie. The entire community is harmed. Why? Because sexual sins—like all sins—cannot be contained within an illusory private sphere. Our lives are intertwined—deeply within family but also within the community. If you doubt this, just think about the problems a troublesome neighbor causes you.

Or think of the social impact of such other "private" sins, such as, drunkenness, drug abuse, broken families or compulsive gambling. If your neighbor is doing these things, he is not loving his neighbor. Why? Because he is degrading the neighborhood. And the more the neighbors are doing these things, the worse the neighborhood is going to be.

This is why the rules—and the politics that lead to them—are important.

Something Greater is Ahead

What occurs in the kingdom of the world is a reflection of the spiritual realities at stake. There are eternal consequences to right and wrong and good and evil. Every sin, after all, is not only against man but, more significantly, against God.

And it is no coincidence that those who seek to evade God's absolute justice are the ones who want to subvert earthly justice. "Love must conquer all," they say…meaning that the punishment of earthly transgressions must be reduced or excused altogether. "After all, isn't this the loving thing to do?" And to be religious about it, "Isn't God a God of love? How could a loving God punish someone forever? Surely he will overlook the sinner's sins, won't he?"

No, he won't.

LOVE AND JUSTICE

God is love and he is just. To eliminate one or the other is to deny who God is. It is to create a false God, a "nice" God, an idol.

So how are love and justice fully reconciled?

Errrr...

I don't know either. But both are demonstrated on the cross. Love *and* justice. The love of Jesus does not eliminate justice, but pays its full penalty. Both are received through faith. You have to believe what God has said and done. This faith is exemplified by Abraham, the "father of all who believe."

> That is why his [Abraham's] faith was "counted to him as righteousness." But the words "it was counted to him" were not written for his sake alone, but for ours also. It will be counted to us who believe in him who raised from the dead Jesus our Lord, who was delivered up for our trespasses and raised for our justification.
>
> Romans 4:22-25

Here is a wonder. The one who rose from the dead, who is the Son of God, who has been appointed by God the Father to judge all things, is the same one who has paid the penalty that his own judgement requires. And for those who believe this good news, Jesus—the Lamb, the Lion, the Judge, the King—will say...

> Come, you who are blessed by my Father, inherit the kingdom prepared for you from the foundation of the world.
>
> Matthew 25:34

* * *

I have made the case that loving your neighbor includes loving your neighborhood. You are not only responsible for your individual-to-individual behavior but also for the good of the larger community. That is, you should work to promote just rulers and just rules. And if your obligations to both your neighbor and your neighborhood seem to be at odds with each other, they are not.

In the final chapter, I will take a closer look at the rules. An understanding of the rules ties all of the various themes related to politics together.

26 Law and Justice

A lawyer asked Jesus a question.

> Teacher, which is the great commandment in the Law?
> Matthew 22:36

What law was he referring to?
Moses' law. Read the context, as you always say.
Correct. But doesn't that surprise you?
No…uh…why should it?
Because Rome ruled Palestine.

Moses' Law

Only once in human history has God imparted a comprehensive system of law. This body of law addressed all aspects of life, including civil law, the rules for public order. This was the law given through Moses. It is summarized in the Ten Commandments and detailed further throughout Moses' books.

Moses' law is in the legal form of a covenant. A covenant is simply an agreement between parties.

The Bible is a book of covenants. You cannot understand the Bible without understanding its covenants. Who are the parties in a covenant? What is God's purpose for a covenant? And how are the covenants related to each other?

There are two big covenants in the Bible—big in the sense that they have a large amount of text dedicated to them. We label the major sections of the Bible along this line—the Old Testament and the New Testament. "Testament" is another word for "covenant."

Moses is central to the Old Covenant. Jesus is central to the New.

Every covenant defines the obligations and responsibilities of the parties to the covenant. The terms and conditions of the Old Covenant are contained in Moses' law. Obedience or disobedience to this law resulted in God's blessings or curses.

Which nation was bound by the Old Covenant? Or are all nations obligated to abide by its terms and conditions? The answer is not difficult. Moses' law/Old Covenant/Old Testament was a contract between God and one nation. Israel. Read Exodus chapter twenty-four if you doubt this. Moses' law distinguished the covenant people from all the other peoples on the earth.

This covenant dominated and determined Israel's history. It is even in their poetry.

> He declares his word to Jacob,
> his statutes and rules to Israel.
> He has not dealt thus with any other nation;
> they do not know his rules.
>
> Psalm 147:19-20

How did Israel fare under the Old Covenant with its code of Moses' law?

Not well.

Most of the Old Testament is the historical record of Israel's national disobedience to this covenant, although punctuated now and again by the faithfulness of certain individuals. The prophetic books may be summarized as a collection of encouragements and warnings regarding the covenant. Encouragement to receive God's blessings through obedience. Warning of God's curses for disobedience.

One of the curses resulting from disobedience was that the Jews would be ruled by foreigners. Which brings me back to Roman rule.

Russian Dolls

Rome allowed varying levels of self-government in the nations they conquered, which is the way empires prefer to do it. More cost effective, less troublesome. But there were always limits. For example, the Jewish leaders could impose certain penalties but were required to bring Jesus before Pilate in order to obtain capital punishment. And when the Apostle Paul was the focus of a riot in Jerusalem, the Roman military quickly took control of the situation.

So in Jesus' and the apostles' day there were two sets of national rulers and two sets of rules. Like those wooden Russian dolls that fit inside of each other, Jewish law was confined within Roman law. As long as the Jews paid their taxes and maintained public order the Romans allowed the Jews to govern themselves as they chose. And they chose to govern themselves in accordance with Moses' law.

Sort of.

There was an inherent conflict in this arrangement. Do you see it? Moses' law was not merely "religious" law that fit nicely within a foreign civil law. Moses' law was the complete package. So the Jews' challenge was to figure how to submit to both Moses and Caesar. It took some slippery lawyering to deconflict them, which is why Roman taxes were a hot issue. Should they pay or not pay? Was it permitted?

The Jews soon tired of all these legal complexities and forced compromises. They desired to throw off the Roman yoke and govern themselves fully. To achieve this, they thought that two things were necessary. They must obey Moses' law to the extent possible. Then, in turn, God would send a messiah to deliver them from bondage.

Which brings me back to Jesus.

The Surprising Messiah

Jesus is God's messiah…but he was not the one the Jews expected. For one thing, he did not dispatch the Romans. For another, he did not interpret Moses according to convention.

Now the lawyer's question to Jesus once more. This time with the answer.

> And one of them, a lawyer, asked him a question to test him. "Teacher, which is the great commandment in the Law?" And he said to him, "You shall love the Lord your God with all your heart and with all your soul and with all your mind. This is the great and first commandment. And a second is like it: You shall love your neighbor as yourself. On these two commandments depend all the Law and the Prophets."
>
> Matthew 22:35-40

If I had not read his answer, I would have wagered my money that the great commandment was one of the Ten Commandments. After all, those were the big ones, weren't they? But Jesus was a better Moses' scholar than I. The lawyer even admitted that he was right.

LAW AND JUSTICE

Lovers Old and New

When Jesus answered the lawyer's question he was not creating some novel interpretation of Moses. He was quoting him.

> You shall love the LORD your God with all your heart and with all your soul and with all your might.
>
> Deuteronomy 6:5

> You shall not take vengeance or bear a grudge against the sons of your own people, but you shall love your neighbor as yourself.
>
> Leviticus 19:18

Neither Moses nor Jesus was imposing new commandments. They were summarizing the objective of all the commandments, which is to love God and neighbor.

Consider some differences between the great commandments and all the rest, which I will call the "lesser" commandments.

The great commandments are "shalls." The lesser commandments are "shall-nots."[30] The great commandments are directed at the inward affection of the heart. The lesser commandments are directed at the outward actions of the body. The great commandments are universal rules in the everlasting kingdom. The lesser commandments are specific rules in the kingdom of the world.

Do these distinctions mean that the great and lesser commandments are opposed to each other? Are they mutually exclusive? No. They are both expressions of God's moral standards. Do what is good. Don't do what is evil.

The greater commandments, however, are more demanding than the lesser commandments. Much more demanding.

> You have heard that it was said to those of old, "You shall not murder; and whoever murders will be liable to judgment." But I say to you that everyone who is angry with his brother will be liable to judgment; whoever insults his brother will be liable to the council; and whoever says, "You fool!" will be liable to the hell of fire.
>
> Matthew 5:21-22

---

[30] Even if a lesser commandment is stated positively, such as "You shall honor your father and mother," it is enforced negatively, that is, by punishment not reward. See Deuteronomy 21:18-21.

The love standard is broader and deeper than the rules that man must make to maintain the social order.

The "but" that begins the second sentence does not mean Jesus is eliminating man's laws against murder, which are lesser commandments. He is saying that God will judge—Jesus himself will judge—not only the physical act of murder "but" also the desire to murder, which is expressed in anger and in words. He is greatly expanding the crime of murder to include the thoughts and intentions of the heart. And Jesus applies this standard across all thoughts and actions—adultery, lying, etc.

Anything that falls short of the love commandments is disobedience to God's everlasting rule, although it may not violate man's limited rule. Man is only able to judge what is physical, what is outward. This, by the way, is the standard by which people prefer to judge themselves. The Jewish leaders, for example, were experts in this department, which drew some pointed commentary from Jesus.

> Woe to you, scribes and Pharisees, hypocrites! For you tithe mint and dill and cumin, and have neglected the weightier matters of the law: justice and mercy and faithfulness. These you ought to have done, without neglecting the others.
>
> Matthew 23:23

They strictly kept to the letter of lesser commandments while ignoring the intent of the great ones.

It is so tempting to pile on here. But I am hesitant to cast stones at the Jewish leaders...because my own failings in this area will be exposed someday.

Fulfillment

Before I move on from this concept of the greater and lesser commandments, there is an important word that summarizes the connection between them.

Fulfill.

Jesus used this word to describe his relationship to Moses' law. He fulfilled it.[31] There many facets to Moses' law in addition to providing civil order—the sacrifices, the holy days, the uniqueness of the covenant people, prophecies, and blessings and curses. They were all brought to completion or fully realized in Jesus.

---

[31] See Matthew 5:17-18.

The Apostle Paul used this same word in that great passage on politics, Romans chapter thirteen.

Long ago, at the beginning of this book, I examined the first half of this passage. If you summon all of your mental powers, you will recall that these verses are about authority. All authority is from God, including government ruling authority. The kingdom of the world derives its authority from the everlasting kingdom. God appoints rulers. Rulers are to rule justly. In return, the ruled are to submit to them.

The second half of the Romans passage is about love and law. Here is how it begins.

> Pay to all what is owed to them: taxes to whom taxes are owed, revenue to whom revenue is owed, respect to whom respect is owed, honor to whom honor is owed. Owe no one anything, except to love each other, for the one who loves another has **fulfilled** the law.
> Romans 13:7-8

Paul uses the word "owe" six times in these two sentences. You owe. That is, you are under obligation to provide something. To government you owe taxes, respect, revenue and honor. This is your duty in the kingdom of the world.

Then the apostle expands from a focus on government to a larger view including all human relationships. "Owe no one anything." Your responsibility to government, you see, is a subset of your general responsibility to all of mankind. What is that responsibility? To love each other.

And if you doubt that Paul is referring to Jesus' second great commandment, the Apostle then uses the word "neighbor" to make sure you see the connection.

> For the commandments, "You shall not commit adultery, You shall not murder, You shall not steal, You shall not covet," and any other commandment, are summed up in this word: "You shall love your **neighbor** as yourself." Love does no wrong to a neighbor; therefore love is the fulfilling of the law.
> Romans 13:9-10

Love does no wrong to a neighbor because love always does what is good for a neighbor. Law prohibits acts that unjustly harm a neighbor. Therefore, if you are motivated by love, you have no need of law to punish you for doing something you will not do. Love, in this sense, fulfills or completes the law. Now, a visual.

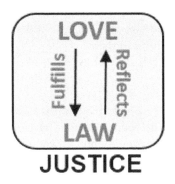

Again, there would be no need for lesser commandments if everyone always loved their neighbor. There would no need for a murder law if no one was murdering anyone. But murder laws are necessary if there are murderers. Murderers are not loving their neighbors. Therefore, justice requires the punishment of the evil doers.

Hold on. You are switching back and forth between Moses' law and a more general concept of law. Which are you talking about?

Both. This is what Paul does in Romans chapter thirteen when he applies Jesus' love-your-neighbor commandment to government.

The church in Rome was probably a largely Gentile congregation, although it included Jewish members. Regardless, Paul cites the sixth, seventh, eight and tenth commandments of Moses' law to Roman Christians, who are under the New Covenant not the Old. Why? Because these lesser commandments reflect the great commandments, which are applicable to all.

Having said that, it is important to remember what Moses' law or any other code of law in the kingdom of the world cannot do.

Justice Not Justification

Paul writes in the strongest terms that law-keeping will never make anyone righteous before God. Here is one sample.

> Yet we know that a person is not justified by works of the law but through faith in Jesus Christ, so we also have

> believed in Christ Jesus, in order to be justified by faith in Christ and not by works of the law, because by works of the law no one will be justified.
>
> Galatians 2:16

The problem with law-keeping is not that you keep some of it some of the time. It is that you do not keep all of it all of the time. To illustrate, imagine a court scene in which a bank robber is being tried by a judge.

> Robber: *Well, your honor, I kept the speed limit both to and from the bank. And—I think this is very significant—I even paid the parking meter in front of the bank.*
>
> Judge: *And what of the detail of robbing the bank.*
>
> Robber: *There is that. But on the whole, I think those two positive marks outweigh the negative one.*

The point? Nobody keeps all of the lesser commandments, much less the great ones. All are lawbreakers.

So if the law condemns you and everyone else, should you hate it? No. You should love it.

Law Lovers

The condemnation of the law discredits the one who can never save you. Yourself. And leads you to the one who can. Jesus. The need for sacrifices foreshadowed this under the Old Covenant. Jesus fulfilled it under the New. This is the biggest reason to love the law.

But there is another. The morality of the law. You should also love the law because it reflects the righteousness of God. Those who loved God under the Old Covenant loved Moses' law. Listen to the Psalmist.

> Teach me, O LORD, the way of your statutes;
> and I will keep it to the end.
> Give me understanding, that I may keep your law
> and observe it with my whole heart.
> Lead me in the path of your commandments,
> for I delight in it.
>
> Psalm 119:33-35

This is an Old Testament expression of the desire to obey and honor God. Here is how Jesus said it in the New.

> Whoever has my commandments and keeps them, he it is who loves me.
>
> John 14:21

I am still getting confused about all the different concepts of law that you are mixing together. Are you talking about Moses' law or Jesus' law or Roman law?

All of them.

While these laws have their distinctions, they also have three things in common. Authority. Justice. And judgement.

Authority

All laws are based upon God's authority as ruler of the everlasting kingdom. There is no authority apart from God's authority. God has delegated authority to rule over the earth to Adam's race. Man rules under God.

That is simple enough on the whole, but the question of jurisdiction arises. Which rules apply to whom? Which rules are authoritative for whom? I'll review them one at a time.

Moses' law. Only Israel was under the Old Covenant. Christians never have been. Nor has anyone else. Consider Sabbath observance, for example. This was mandatory under Moses' law and the Jews brought national curses upon themselves for their Sabbath violations. But no other people or nation has or will be judged for failing to keep Moses' Sabbath laws.

Next, Jesus' law. Love God, love neighbor. Who is required to obey the great commandments? Everyone. All people of all times. Why? Because they are rooted in the character of the Creator and the obligation of the created to rule the earth. The great commandments are the laws which will measure every individual at the final and eternal judgement. Jesus will pronounce his verdict on every thought, action and intention of the heart.

Finally, Roman law. This was the legal system of the Roman empire, which was the ruling power during the time of the New Testament writings. Since Rome has passed from the historical scene, their law no longer applies to you or anyone else. Zero jurisdiction presently.

However, the biblical teaching to those living under Rome also applies in whatever political situation you find yourself. Rulers are to do good and punish evil. Rules are to be just. The ruled are to submit to and support rulers and rules. Surprisingly, perhaps, your responsibilities under the current "Rome" were modeled by Old Covenant Jews subjected to foreign rule. Remember the political efforts of Joseph, Daniel, Esther and Mordecai.

Justice

Moses' law was the law of the land for Israel, but it demonstrated justice to other nations.

> See, I have taught you statutes and rules, as the LORD my God commanded me, that you should do them in the land that you are entering to take possession of it. Keep them and do them, for that will be your wisdom and your understanding in the sight of the peoples, who, when they hear all these statutes, will say, 'Surely this great nation is a wise and understanding people.' ...And what great nation is there, that has statutes and rules so righteous as all this law that I set before you today?
> Deuteronomy 4:5-8

However, as I mentioned before, not everything in Moses' law defined civil order. It also served to distinguish Israel as God's covenant people by laws requiring Sabbath observance, putting tassels on clothing and not eating unclean animals, for example. These were only authoritative for the Old Covenant Jews.

Furthermore, when the Judaizers taught that New Covenant Christians were required to keep Moses' law in order to be saved, Paul refuted them in the strongest language.

Why then did Paul in Romans chapter thirteen cite the sixth, seventh, eighth and tenth commandments—which prohibit murder, adultery, theft and coveting—as applicable to the church? Because these are fulfilled by the universal love-your-neighbor commandment, which is binding on all people. And Christians of all people should reflect the moral righteousness of God—not to earn salvation but because they have been transformed by it.

While the laws of Moses could not justify the Jews, it did save them the trouble of having to make their own rules. When God writes your laws, you can be assured that the lesser commandments will be in sync with the greater ones. Everyone else in the kingdom of the world has had to do the work themselves.

Along for the Ride

There is one more thing that Moses' law, Jesus' law and Roman law have in common. The violation of them incurs God's judgement.

There is God's future eternal judgement, the final and comprehensive verdict of Jesus. This will be a judgement of individuals. Here every person will stand alone in the docket and be tried for what he has done in relation to the great commandments. I am not referring to that one. There is also a present judgement of individuals. Although you may question God's timing and execution of this, actions have consequences. Now. A man will reap what he sows. But I am not referring to that judgement either.

The judgement I want to focus on is both present and collective. It is the judgement not of an individual but of a group—a group defined by rulers, rules and the ruled. In other words, a political organization. And when God brings judgement upon a nation, state, clan, whatever, everyone in that group will suffer.

Wait a minute! If my politics are right, if I am doing what is good and resisting evil, why should I be punished along with the evildoers?

Because you are a member of a people, a community. And wherever that bus goes, you are along for the ride, whether you are willing or not.

But to the larger question, if you doubt that God judges all nations, review the prophetic books. While many of the prophecies concerned Israel and Judah, the other nations also drew God's attention. And what were his charges against those nations? Idolatry. Violence. Cruelty. Oppression. Wickedness. Etc. These are the same sins the Jews were guilty of, less those laws that were solely binding upon the covenant people.

And if you doubt that national judgement effects everyone, ask yourself this: Who escapes it? If a nation suffers, who in the nation suffers? Was righteous Daniel spared from the Babylonian captivity? No. Was Dietrich Bonhoeffer unscathed under Nazi rule? No again. And even if Bonhoeffer had not conspired against Hitler, would he have escaped conflict with that totalitarian government or the destruction of Germany during the war? No and no. Everyone suffers under national judgement.

Judgement Within and Without

Speaking of the Nazis, they illustrate how God judges in the kingdom of the world.

I said at the beginning of this book that it is not only the rulers that are responsible for the rules. The ruled select and support their rulers and the rules they make. One cannot lead if nobody is following.

All peoples have a responsibility to replace their rulers and rules when there is injustice in the land. The greater the injustice, the greater the motivation for change. Why? Because the more people that are forced to taste injustice, the more there are that want to change the menu. It becomes personal. While you may overlook the oppression of others, you will not ignore injustice when it is directed against you.

But replacing rulers is rarely an easy task. Few are willing to step aside without a fight. And the worse the ruler and the more retribution he fears, the greater he will fight. Every attempt by Germans failed to remove Hitler.

Which brings me to the second way God judges nations. If the locals won't clean up their own injustice, God may whistle for others to do the job. Judgement is not only intra-national. It may also be inter-national.

Consider Habakkuk. This Old Testament prophet began his book by bemoaning Judah's iniquity, destruction, violence, strife and contention. Then he makes this observation about law and justice.

> So the law is paralyzed, and justice never goes forth. For the wicked surround the righteous; so justice goes forth perverted.
>
> Habakkuk 1:4

That is quite an indictment.
God responds.

> Look among the nations, and see; wonder and be astounded. For I am doing a work in your days
> that you would not believe if told.
>
> Habakkuk 1:5

God is going to do something. And he is going to do it with an outside hire. "Look among the nations."

You must remember that God had equipped the Jews for justice more than any other people. They had Moses' law. They had the prophets to both warn and encourage them. They had the lessons of their own history. And yet "the law is paralyzed and justice never goes forth."

Who will God choose among the nations to bring his judgement upon Judah?

> For behold, I am raising up the Chaldeans, that bitter and hasty nation, who march through the breadth of the earth, to seize dwellings not their own. They are dreaded and fearsome; their justice and dignity go forth from themselves.
>
> Habakkuk 1:6-7

The Chaldeans were the Babylonians. Hmmm. Interesting choice. Note especially that last phrase, "Their justice and dignity go forth from themselves." Interpretation: *They ignore God's laws*.

The Babylonians are not portrayed as virtuous champions of justice. They are a marauding pack of thieves who "seize dwellings not their own." Nevertheless, God uses them to accomplish his purposes. The everlasting kingdom rules over the kingdom of the world.

Habakkuk then raised a second complaint. He was never satisfied, it seems, and somewhat of a whiner. To summarize, he said, "They are more evil than we are! What's up with that?" God answered that he would give the Babylonians their just desserts in due time.

So God used the wickeder Babylonians to judge the wicked Israelites. In the case of Hitler's Germany, the Soviet communists were at least as bad as the Nazis. They were worse by many measures. The other Allied nations were not pure either. But they were amateurs compared to the injustices committed by those two totalitarian nations.

What is going on here?

God's judgement of a nation by other nations may also be his judgement on those other nations. None are blameless. The rod that gives a beating takes a beating while giving it. Conflict is painful for all.

Bottom Line: The kingdom of the world operates within the sovereign rule of God—a God who exercises judgement upon all nations in accordance with justice. If a people will not rule themselves as they should, the Judge may bring in others to impose the penalty. And that is usually more painful.

So you have a vested interest in just laws. And if you won't work for justice in the land for yourself, at least do it for your neighbor.

* * *

I realize that this too has been a challenging chapter, which is why I saved it for the end. I have attempted to show the full tapestry of the Bible's law teaching as it is woven together. If any threads are left out or misaligned, the overall design will be incomplete or distorted.

This completes my examination of rulers, rules and the ruled and your political responsibilities within the kingdom of the world. Which means that I should wrap it up.

Conclusion

You have traveled a long journey through a short book—rulers/rules/the ruled, the Dominion Mandate, the institutions of government, family and employment, the four kingdoms, the role of a church, a featured cast of political operatives, conscience, religion, love, law and justice.

My hope is that you will fully embrace your roles and responsibilities in the kingdom of the world. This is a theme that is woven throughout the Bible's teaching. It is displayed in the lives of godly men and women. And it is contrary to today's cultural currents that pressure you to withdraw your public influence. While I have focused on politics, I have also mentioned the areas of family and employment. Your obligation to rule well is the same for all three authority structures. God has given you a job to do and you should do it. All of it.

Throughout the history of Christianity some have tried to avoid politics and other dominion duties. These are the separatists of one flavor or another. Some got off track by equating the kingdom of Satan with the kingdom of the world, assuming that matter is evil and that which is spiritual is good. The path to holiness, accordingly, is to avoid the world and all its entanglements.

The separatists should have been better readers of their Bibles. There is both good and evil in the spiritual realm. And while the physical world was corrupted by man's fall, it is not evil. It is not dirt but sin that soils you.

Most Christians have not been separatists. The hard work of evading what we were created to do is not for everyone. The main contribution of the separatists has been to confuse the rest of us about what godly living looks like.

But it is not only these voices inside the church telling you to shirk politics. The secularists on the outside are telling you this as well. Their pitch is that you are not allowed to let your "religious" ideas intrude upon the "rational" business of politics. *Keep your morality to yourself...so that we can impose ours.*

Both the separatists and the secularists arrive at the same destination, although by different roads. *The political arena is no place for Christianity.* The separatists want you to remain "unstained by the world." The secularists want to silence your biblical morality when it opposes their beliefs.

But all people stand on common ground. The yearning for a just society proves that we are all image bearers of God. This is why everyone wraps their politics in justice talk. Power plays are not enough. Everything must be justified. But all that is justified is not just. Conscience may be deceived. Evil may be called good and good evil. Politics will be either one or the other.

* * *

Before I end, I must revisit a few other ideas that I stumbled across along the path of my main theme. I will mention them again in case you missed them the first time around. And since I am mentioning them, I might as well squeeze some more juice out of them. After these few thoughts, I will trouble you no more.

* * *

You may have noticed that I have not used the term "social justice" in this book. Not once. Until now.

I have been sorely tempted to use it. After all, justice in society is what God commands. It is the goal of good politics. So what is wrong with social justice? The problem is that it has come to mean something else. And there is a lie in that something else.

What makes the lie so effective is that it is wrapped in truth. The truth is that some people, because of their group identity, oppress other people, because of their group identity. *It is us against them.* And so there are victims and oppressors. And sometimes the tables are turned and the victims become the oppressors. This cannot be denied. It happens. All the time. Throughout history.

Politics naturally feeds upon group identification. Why? Because the easiest way to round up voters is to form them into a herd. *You are a member of my group and I am the champion of your cause.* I do not criticize here. It is not always a bad thing. A group may promote either justice or injustice.

And now the lie. The lie is that the state should administer justice on the basis of group identity through the lens of victim oppression. It is guilt or innocence by association. It is disadvantage or advantage according to classification. It is judgement by statistics. And it is deeply corrupting.

While injustice may be dished out collectively, justice must be served individually. That is, rulers should judge according to what a person has done, not according to what others have done. Why? Because injustice is always personal. It boils down to someone harming someone else.

Imagine a gang fight between the Reds and the Blues. During the melee one of the Reds kills a Blue. The background is that the Reds and Blues have been knocking off each other for some time. The Reds hate the Blues

CONCLUSION

and the Blues return the favor.

What does justice require? Are all of the Reds guilty of murder? No. The one who killed is. Should the murder be excused because of a long violent history with the Blues? No again. Should the state judge the motives of the murderer's heart? Three times no. Why? Because only God can do that. The penalty for deliberate, premeditated murder should be for what was done, not for the prejudice that was underneath the doing of it.

A law should apply equally to everyone. Otherwise it will give advantage to some while disadvantaging others. This is, by definition, unfair. A law that applies to all may be unjust to all, but a law that does not is always unjust to some. Everyone should play under the same set of rules.

There is something underneath these two approaches to justice—group guilt versus individual guilt. This is somebody's religion, of course. It is a belief about the nature of man. The difference between plain old justice and social justice is that the first is grounded in the belief that each person is a moral being who is ultimately responsible for his behavior. The problem is that there is evil in the man. The second assumes that people are largely products of their environment. They are like corks being carried along on a river. The river is at fault. It is the river that must be rerouted.

And in case you haven't noticed, social justice theory has broadened lately.

The older social justice was based on physical characteristics and associations. Race, ethnicity, class, sex. These are the circumstances in which you find yourself. The newer social justice is based upon behavior, specifically sexual behavior. The new has cloaked itself as the old in an attempt to obscure the difference. But skin pigment, for example, is not a moral issue, while sexual practice is.

All societies make rules about sex. Why? Because rules are about what you do and how it affects others. And few things affect others more personally and socially than sex. The political struggle is over what the rules should be, not if there should be rules.

There is another deception hidden within the new social justice. It is that the problem with immoral behavior is those who oppose it. Guilt and shame are the fault of others. If everyone approved of the behavior, then those who practice it would be happy. But the problem is not external, especially not with those who speak the truth in love. The problem is internal. It is conscience that condemns such behavior. And those who try to silence their conscience through their political activism will be sorely disappointed with the results, not only now but at the final judgement.

And speaking of the final judgement, it will not be conducted in accordance with current social justice doctrine. While Jesus will gather the nations, he will not judge them as nations. You will not be crowded into the docket as a Bulgarian or Mongolian or Mexican or American. You will stand in the docket alone. Nationality (or any other grouping) will not matter. Morality will. Jesus will separate the "sheep from the goats," the blessed from the cursed.[32]

There is a great dignity but also a fearsome accountability in bearing the image of God and in being entrusted to rule the earth. When our first parents sinned, their defense was to blame on someone else. This has been the human tendency ever since. But outside influences notwithstanding, each person is still responsible for his actions.

Justice demands it.

* * *

Do you feel guilty about the scope of your political involvement? Maybe you should. Maybe you shouldn't.

My intent has not been to laden you with guilt. It has been for you to fulfill your kingdom-of-the-world duties. All of them. In obedience to God and as an expression of your faith.

But just because everyone has ruler-ruled responsibilities does not mean that everyone has the same responsibilities. This depends upon your gifts and abilities and your strengths and weaknesses.

It also depends upon the circumstances that God brings about. I don't think young Joseph was aspiring to be Pharaoh's number two when he was strutting around in that fancy coat. Regarding myself, I have no intention of becoming an activist or running for office. I am not suited for it. I could do a lot of damage…and probably would.

Some of you, however, are made to serve and honor God in these ways. You understand the times. You have a moral clarity about the issues of the day. You enjoy the public spotlight and are energized by the political arena. If so, go for it.

And if you are aiming at the right things—as far as I can tell—I will support you. I will not be quick to criticize you in the wheeling-and-dealing that is inherent in politics. I will expect you to fight against injustices but not to defeat them all at once. Why? Because I know it is difficult and often messy.

I will give you some grace in your vocation…if you give me some in mine.

* * *

---

[32] See Matthew 25:31-46.

CONCLUSION

And one last thing. There is an unending spiritual battle between good and evil, between truth and lies, between loving your neighbor and hating him, and between justice and injustice.

You may think that today is a time of unprecedented peril, divisiveness, and degeneration. It is not. Our moment is not extraordinary. It is ordinary. If you doubt this, read more history. Or if you are an older person, gazing back toward the golden glow of yesteryear, try to remember that the "good old days" were not so good. You may have been unaware of this in your youth. Or you may have just forgotten all that was going on during the moment. The moral struggle always continues, although each age presents its own particular context.

But don't fall off of the other side of the horse, thinking that today's battles are unimportant or futile. They are not. Things may get worse. But they may get better too. And it may be as important to fight and lose as it is to fight and win.

* * *

Love God. Love your neighbor. Your politics should reflect both.

When one rules justly over men,
ruling in the fear of God,
he dawns on them like the morning light,
like the sun shining forth on a cloudless morning,
like rain that makes grass to sprout from the earth.

David (II Samuel 23:3-4)

Acknowledgements

My hero in the fable *The Emperor's New Clothes* is the child. I like him because he states the obvious. "But the emperor has nothing on at all!" That is a role I have attempted to play for you in this book. I am vain enough to think that I have done that. But I am also realistic enough to realize I may not have. So I sought out some honest fellows who are wise and good thinkers and asked them to critique *my* wardrobe. This they did. And the book is better for it. Thank you Chuck Graham, Eric Smith, Javier Mazzetti, Jordan Goodrich, Doug Goodin and Erik Van Os. You have made me appear smarter than I am…or at least you tried.

About the Author

Robert L. Franck writes about Christianity, culture and the interplay between the two. Reasoning from the Bible's teaching, he draws applications for contemporary thought and life. While he is writing primarily for those who submit to biblical authority, others will gain insight into Christian beliefs and practices beyond the usual caricatures. In his quest to persuade and not merely inform the reader, Mr. Franck pens a lively style that engages, entertains and is somewhat provocative.

* * *

ALSO BY ROBERT L. FRANCK

Buy A Cabin: The Theology and Practice of Rest
Franck Words: An Honest Dictionary

* * *

Visit his website at: slowthoughts.com.

Made in the USA
Monee, IL
05 June 2020